Contents

Glocal Pharma

International brands and the imagination of local masculinity

Ericka Johnson, Ebba Sjögren and Cecilia Åsberg

Routledge
Taylor & Francis Group
LONDON AND NEW YORK

First published 2016 by Routledge

2 Park Square, Milton Park, Abingdon, Oxfordshire OX14 4RN
52 Vanderbilt Avenue, New York, NY 10017

Routledge is an imprint of the Taylor & Francis Group, an informa business

First issued in paperback 2020

British Library Cataloguing in Publication Data
A catalogue record for this book is available from the British Library

Library of Congress Cataloging-in-Publication Data
The LOC data has been applied for.

ISBN: 978-1-4724-8163-4 (hbk)
ISBN: 978-0-367-59658-3 (pbk)

Typeset in Times New Roman
by Apex CoVantage, LLC

Glocal Pharma

An exploration of how global pharmaceutical products are localized – of what happens when they become 'glocal' – this book examines the tensions that exist between a global pharmaceutical market and the locally bounded discourses and regulations encountered as markets are created for new drugs in particular contexts. Employing the case study of the emergence, representation and regulation of Viagra in the Swedish market, *Glocal Pharma* offers analyses of commercial material, medical discourses and legal documents to show how a Swedish, Viagra-consuming subject has been constructed in relation to the drug and how Viagra is imagined in relation to the Swedish man.

Engaging with debates about pharmaceuticalization, the authors consider the ways in which new identities are created around drugs, the redefinition of health problems as sits of pharmaceutical treatment and changes in practices of governance to reflect the entrance of pharmaceuticals to the market. With attention to 'local' contexts, it reveals elements in the nexus of pharmaceutcalization that are receptive to cultural elements as new products become embedded in local markets.

An empirically informed study of the ways in which the presence of a drug can alter the concept of a disease and its treatment, understandings of who suffers from it and how to cure it – both locally and internationally – this book will appeal to scholars of sociology and science and technology studies with interests in globalization, pharmaceuticals, gender and the sociology of medicine.

Ericka Johnson is Assistant Director of the Technology and Social Change Division at Linköping University, Sweden and co-editor of *Technology and Medical Practice: Blood, Guts and Machines*.

Ebba Sjögren is Associate Professor in the Department of Accounting at Stockholm School of Economics, Sweden.

Cecilia Åsberg is Associate Professor and Head of Gender Studies at Linköping University, Sweden.

Global Connections
Series Editor: Robert Holton, Trinity College, Dublin

Global Connections builds on the multidimensional and continuously expanding interest in globalization. The main objective of the series is to focus on 'connectedness' and provide readable case studies across a broad range of areas such as social and cultural life and economic, political and technological activities.

The series aims to move beyond abstract generalities and stereotypes: 'Global' is considered in the broadest sense of the word, embracing connections between different nations, regions and localities, including activities that are transnational and trans-local in scope; 'Connections' refers to movements of people, ideas, resources and all forms of communication as well as the opportunities and constraints faced in making, engaging with and sometimes resisting globalization. The series is interdisciplinary in focus and publishes monographs and collections of essays by new and established scholars. It fills a niche in the market for books that make the study of globalization more concrete and accessible.

For a full list of titles in this series, please visit www.routledge.com/series/ASHSER1306

Also published in this series:

Violence and Gender in the Globalized World: The Intimate and the Extimate
Edited by Sanja Bahun and V. G. Julie Rajan

Global Exposure in East Asia: A Comparative Study of Microglobalization
Ming-Chang Tsai

Global Inequalities beyond Occidentalism
Manuela Boatcă

Global Knowledge Production in the Social Sciences: Made in Circulation
Edited by Wiebke Keim, Ercüment Çelik, Christian Ersche and Veronika Wöhrer

Notes on contributors

Ericka Johnson is a Senior Lecturer at the Department of Thematic Studies, Technology and Social Change. Her research has looked at medical technologies and their relationship to the patient body and gender, with a particular focus on pharmaceuticals. Currently she is working on discursive constructions of the ageing prostate. Her publications include the edited volume *Technology and Medical Practice: Blood, Guts and Machines* (with Boel Berner 2010), Ashgate, and *Dreaming of a Mail Order Husband* (2007), Duke University Press.

Ebba Sjögren is Associate Professor at the Department of Accounting, Stockholm School of Economics. Her research centres on the role of knowledge-based management tools in organizational control and decision-making, notably in the health care sector, and the practical undertaking of valuation work in the construction of markets. She combines these two interests in an ongoing cross-country comparative study of price formation and assessment of inpatient pharmaceuticals. Her work has previously been published in journals including *European Accounting Review*, *Journal of Common Market Studies*, *The Sociological Review*, *Valuation Studies* and *Governance*.

Cecilia Åsberg is Professor in Gender Studies at the Department of Thematic Studies at Linköping University. Focusing on reciprocity and vulnerability as a more-than-human condition, she has published on the natures and cultures of genetics, Alzheimer's disease, pharmaceuticals, laboratory life and environed bodies. Currently working on toxic embodiment, she heads a Swedish research programme in environmental humanities. Her most recent book is *A Feminist Companion to the Posthumanities* (with Rosi Braidotti 2015), Springer.

Acknowledgements

This book is a result of interdisciplinary discussions and collaborative writing practices between the three authors and our colleagues in many different academic fields and constellations. We each came to the material from our own disciplines and have also brought with us critics and conversation partners from different places and perspectives. In addition, we have been invited to put chapter drafts forward in many different seminar groups, which has been invaluable. Thank you to all of you who have helped us find our way through this project! In particular, we would like to thank Boel Berner, Elin Björk, Maria Björkman, Anna Bredström, Jelmer Brüggemann, Oscar Javier Maldonado Casteneda, Isabelle Dussauge, Mark Elam, Kathrin Friedrich, Andreas Gunnarsson, Lisa Guntram, Ali Hanbury, Katherine Harrison, Marie-Louise Holm, Klasien Horstman, Ine van Hoyweghen, Sari Irni, Sonja Jerak-Zuiderent, Marianne Winther Jörgensen, Corinna Kruse, Bengt Larsson, Francis Lee, Marin Letell, Lisa Lindén, Sebastian Linke, Nina Lykke, Erik Malmqvist, Tara Mehrabi, Ulf Mellström, Shai Mulinari, Alma Persson, Anders Persson, Jesper Petersson, Celia Roberts, Kerstin Sandell, Göran Sundqvist, Håkan Thörn, Steve Woolgar, Kristin Zeiler and Teun Zuiderent-Jerak.

We would also like to thank the funders who have made large parts of this work possible: the Swedish Science Council, which financed the project 'Culture, biomedicalization and changing masculinities: Viagra™ as symbol and technology', the European Research Council under the European Union's Seventh Framework Programme (FP7/2007–2013)/ERC grant agreement no. 263657, PPPHS, and the Jan Wallander and Tom Hedelius Foundation. In addition, the project has benefitted from institutional support at The Swedish Collegium for Advanced Study, Gothenburg University, Stockholm School of Economics and, primarily, Linköping University.

1 Introduction

Glocal pharmaceuticalization

Ericka Johnson

The pharmaceutical nexus is large, international and successful. It is also very complex. Heterogeneous in its components, stretching both upstream to research, clinical trials, product development and disease construction, and downstream through doctors and experts, it enables and enrols regulatory bodies, lawmakers, lobbyists, judicial systems, marketing professionals, producers, medical practitioners and consumers. And it does this on a global scale, dominating the medical approach in advanced Western countries and spreading its territory to domains in the developing world. Pharmaceuticals are colonizing and creating new markets in geographically and socially diverse parts of the world and throughout all aspects of the industry. The pharmaceutical industry is trying, and succeeding, to work and profit in very different contexts, with very different regulatory frameworks, marketing needs and consumer bases. And while the industry has had an international approach since before World War II, the global market for pharmaceuticals and the profit margins, which large, multinational companies are chasing, have grown exponentially in recent decades.

These themes are prevalent in critical studies of global pharmaceuticals from within the social sciences (see Elliot 2003; Moynihan and Cassels 2005; Petryna and Kleinman 2006; Williams *et al.* 2011a). In this book, we present a close look at the glocal of global pharma in Sweden. By attending to the specificities of the local in Sweden within a conceptual framework of global pharmaceuticals, we will be showing global trends and local responses in a Western/Northern, highly developed and regulated state. To do so, we employ the term *glocal* to signify that the local specificities of a cultural context, including its regulatory bodies, do something to the global pharmaceuticals that are integrated into it, and, likewise, global pharmaceuticals impact the local context.

Critical studies of pharmaceuticals have developed out of academic work on medicalization, a concept often traced back to work inspired by Parsons's analysis of the sick role in the 1950s. Medicalization became a sociological tool with which to think about the interplay between medicine, individuals and society. Parsons's proposition, that the sick role allows the individual to avoid blame for his/her illness while simultaneously legitimating and excusing his/her shortcomings in the workplace or family as long as the individual seeks medical help (Parsons 1951), has resonated throughout medical sociology and influenced the development of the field since. Within sociology, studies of medicalization initially focused on the hospital as a professional institution within which the patient figured, but where doctors (and to a lesser extent, nurses) were particularly interesting to study as they assumed professional roles, made decisions, directed practice and policy and (almost peripherally) attended the ill (see Eaton and Weil 1955; Balint 1957; Fox 1959; Becker *et al.* 1961; Coser 1963; Freidson 1963). One finds echoes of the sick role in Illich (1976), Fox refers to it in her work on medicalization in America (Fox 1977, 15), and current interests in the process of pathologizing emotions (Healy 2004) and behaviour (Hart *et al.* 2006; Conrad 2007) touch on the interplay between illness and society.

How exactly medicalization occurs is, of course, up for debate, as is what should be included in the term. Illich famously called it '*iatrogenesis*', combining the Greek *iatros*, 'physician', and *genesis*, 'origin' (Illich 1976, 3), yet it is used to convey a very broad set of processes, sites and actors beyond the physician and his/her workplace. The concept of medicalization has expanded beyond the idea of the sick role, to include ideas of how a patient's complaint becomes a medical diagnosis (Balint 1957), and how social deviance becomes medicalized (cf. Fox 1977). It now applies to 'a process by which nonmedical problems become defined and treated as medical problems, usually in terms of illness and disorders' (Conrad 2007, 4), including, and worryingly, the transformation of difference into pathology (Conrad 2007, 148). Forty years ago, Illich pointed to the way ill health is created by what he termed the *medical bureaucracy*, which defined the need for medical care – defined non-normative ways of being as diseased and in need of medical treatment – and discursively limited the ability or opportunity for other forms of care, be that social, familial, spiritual or self-care (Illich 1976, 40). Critical studies of medicalization in the social sciences today look beyond the immediate medical context to explore how commercial, state and media interests also produce illness. And while, within medical sociology, medicalization is still largely used to direct attention to issues of how illness is understood and used in social contexts, work by Mol (2002) and other science and technology studies (STS) researchers broaches and questions the illness/disease divide, and has begun to approach biomedical technologies with a critical lens (Berg and Mol 1998; Johnson and Berner 2010). These examine how illness and disease are enacted, but also how their particular formations shape medical practice and governance.

Medicalization conceptually sets the stage for the idea of pharmaceuticalization, understood to mean the introduction and acceptance of drug-based responses to (and creation of) health issues, as illustrated in Dumit's (2012) book *Drugs for Life*. Williams, Martin and Gabe use the term *pharmaceuticalization* to interrogate how many different aspects of life are becoming opportunities for pharmaceutical intervention. In their usage, *pharmaceuticalization* is a broad term, and can be applied to processes of 'discovery, development, commercialization, use and governance of pharmaceutical products centred around chemistry-based technology' (Williams *et al.* 2011a, 711). This is opposed to Abraham's more medically focused use of the term (Abraham 2010, 604). In its broader definition, which we embrace in this book, *pharmaceuticalization* can also be applied to the use of pharmaceuticals to address issues currently outside of medical practice, like some lifestyle drugs or the use of nicotine replacement therapies in chewing gum or e-cigarettes (see Elam 2012). This broader stance is not as new or controversial as the Abraham (2011) versus Williams and colleagues (2011b) exchange would suggest. As Illich pointed out long before our current obsession with lifestyle drugs, pharmaceuticals do not need doctors and hospitals to pervade society, nor are most 'poisons', 'remedies' and 'placebos' necessarily destined for the sick (Illich 1976, 61).

Reminding us of pharma's ambiguity, Illich noted: 'The Greek's only word for "drug" – *pharmakon* – did not distinguish between the power to cure and the power to kill' (Illich 1976, 45). While not as radical in their take on pharmaceuticals as Illich, Williams and colleagues point out that both *medicalization* and *pharmaceuticalization* are ostensibly value-neutral terms (Williams *et al.* 2011a, 711), and *medicalization* and *pharmaceuticalization* both describe processes that may imply benefits or drawbacks to society and individuals. But, as has been the case with medicalization, in social science studies of pharmaceuticalization there seems to be a tendency to see these processes as negative, or at least suspicious. Abraham echoes this reticence towards pharmaceuticals when he writes 'that increased pharmaceuticalization can sometimes be suboptimal for significant therapeutic advances in the interests of public health' (Abraham 2010, 603).

The relationship between pharmaceuticalization and medicalization is sometimes very intertwined, and many critical studies of pharmaceuticals have shown how drugs are being used to manufacture diseases which can then be treated with them. But the process of pharmaceuticalization can imply more than just increased medicalization. Many examples exist where pharmaceuticalization changes the method of treating an already existing medical condition. As Abraham notes, 'pharmaceuticalization can grow *without expansion of medicalization*, because some drugs are increasingly used to treat an *established* medical condition involving no transformation of a non-medical problem into a medical one' (Abraham 2010, 605; emphasis in the original). This volume discusses the influence of pharmaceuticalization on the treatment of established medical conditions, as well as on marketing communication and the governance of access to such treatment, using the example of Viagra and the treatment of impotence.

What is the subject of the process of pharmaceuticalization? Williams and colleagues use the term *pharmaceutical regime* to cover the networks of institutions, organizations, actors, artefacts and cultural values one can identify in studies of pharmaceuticalization. Others have used the term *pharmaceutical nexus* (cf. Petryna and Kleinman 2006), and Abraham talks in terms of processes (Abraham 2010). What we take from these discussions is the idea that pharmaceuticals are one actor within a complex and heterogeneous *collectif* (Callon and Law 1995) of actors, institutions and ideas, including clinicians, patients, consumers, regulators, sales reps and marketing departments. This *collectif* of actors notably includes the drugs themselves in very specific technological forms – pills, patches, sticks and shots. We treat these material artefacts as a useful prism to see through and with, to bring into focus and refract various values, ideas and desires that are manifested in and through the drugs we are studying.

The theoretical framework of pharmaceuticalization employs analysis of heterogeneous aspects of pharmaceuticals in society, and can productively be approached from within different disciplines. Because of this, the work in this book is multidisciplinary. It is positioned in social science and cultural studies approaches to pharmaceuticals, and employs theories and terms that attend to the flexibility of pharmaceuticals as medical technologies, especially when they become mobile across countries, regulatory frameworks and value systems (cf. Dugdale 2000; Kruse 2016). Our book can be read as a study of pharmaceuticals at an intersection of political, economic and ethical dimensions (cf. Petryna and Kleinman 2006; Brody 2007). Approaching such a multi-scaled and complex nexus demands an analytical toolbox which is heterogeneous and broad, so we have mixed liberally from our disciplinary backgrounds to create an approach drawing from posthumanities studies, STS and medicine and management and organizational studies. This approach is influenced by the authors' own boundary crossings into and within interdisciplinary fields: gender studies; STS and medicine; and social studies of accounting. We bring with us theoretical and methodological baggage from our respective fields, including a shared interest in the materialities of pharmaceuticalization. Methodologically, our research, like much of that we draw inspiration from, is qualitative, and relies on close readings of visual and written discourses. These discourses are taken from regulatory contexts (legal and court documents), professional debates (medical journals and testimonials from medical experts, court witnesses and committee members) and commercial material (advertisements for the drugs, often on 'informational websites' and other Internet forums, to circumvent the Swedish prohibition on direct-to-consumer (DTC) advertising of prescription pharmaceuticals). The different discourses are then analyzed to trace the glocal contours of Swedish Viagra and the Swedish Viagra man.

Despite our disciplinary promiscuity, or 'theoretical eclecticism' (cf. Williams *et al.* 2011a, 722), and the diversity of material we analyze, the overarching theoretical framework in all three sections of this book can be related to the concept of pharmaceuticalization (Abraham 2011; Williams *et al.* 2011a), from which we garner specific questions to query the shapes and forms that global pharmaceuticals assume as they are integrated into local discourses, and how the discourses and the pharmaceuticals change in the process. Pharmaceuticalization has many aspects. Abraham, for example, argues that it involves dimensions from biomedicalism, medicalization, industry drug promotion, consumerism and the ideology or policy of the regulatory state (Abraham 2010, 606). Williams and colleagues (2011a) identify several more aspects, including the role of the media and the use of drugs outside of the medical domain. In this book, we specifically attend to three aspects of pharmaceuticalization that we think are particularly tangible and visible in the case of Swedish Viagra, yet also relevant to a discussion of glocal pharmaceuticalization. These are: the way pharmaceuticals change forms of governance; the redefinition of health problems as issues with a pharmaceutical solution; and the creation of new techno-social identities around drugs and the way pharmaceuticals become essential actors in relationships between subjects. Our analysis of these aspects in Sweden shows how the local context is an important influence on the process of pharmaceuticalization.

The first aspect of pharmaceuticalization, which we will discuss in this book, is the way *pharmaceuticals reshape forms of governance*. In the global debate, examples of pharma-governance are often related to questions about emerging markets, equitable access, cost and patent protection, with political decisions at the nation state level contravening international decisions and regulations – and sometimes even forcing these regulations to change (see Biehl 2006). However, the presence and influence of international pharmaceuticals is also very tangible in governance decisions and policy responses in established and well-regulated nation states, like Sweden, that have a reputation for being obedient to international treaties and understandings. While our material does not provide examples of patent infringement and black or grey market infringement, it does show a nation state finding new ways of regulating and governing pharmaceutical access and subsidies, changing the role of medical doctors and regulatory decision makers at the point of clinical diagnosis.

Critical studies of pharmaceuticals also discuss *the redefinition of health problems as issues with a pharmaceutical solution* (see Healy 2004; Kassirer 2005; Moynihan and Cassels 2005; Law 2006; Moynihan and Mintzes 2010; Williams *et al.* 2009, 712). As Moynihan notes, this process involves, among other things, examples of how pharmaceutical advertising and regulation turn ordinary ailments into medical problems, present mild symptoms as serious, and treat inter-personal problems as medical (Moynihan and Cassels 2005). Our study of the medical discourses around Viagra show this happening very clearly in the Swedish context. Predictably, impotence became erectile dysfunction, and urology replaced relationship counselling and sex therapy as the site of treatment for erectile problems. Yet because of the ideological framework of the Swedish health care system, Viagra was also discursively connected to diabetes, multiple sclerosis and spinal injuries, which tints the identity of the drug and the Swedish Viagra man in the medical discourse.

The creation of new techno-social identities around drugs

In our analysis of the Swedish patient information pages on pharmaceutical webpages, men, doctors and the partners of men with erectile dysfunction are enrolled into a Viagra discourse which presents them with specific tasks and functions in the recognition of, need for and enabling of Viagra. As Chapters 6 and 7 describe, these roles are similar to patient, doctor and partner identities in North American Viagra advertising yet also tweaked to fit perceived Swedish values and norms. As the concept of pharmaceuticalization would predict, Viagra is positioned as a necessary component in these identities and, important, in the relationships between the subject positions that Viagra facilitates. But the shape and shades of these identities and relationships reflect very traditional understandings of the local culture, an interesting example of glocal identities.

Much of the work on global pharmaceuticals explores encounters between developing, non-Western/Northern countries and a commercial pharmaceutical industry. We see the value of this work, and laud its approach to questions of social justice, equitable access to health care and global commercial forces as they discover and create new markets (see Lakoff 2005). We draw theoretical lessons from these studies. For our work, the most useful studies of this global process examine local manifestations of pharmaceuticals with close, qualitative and ethnographically inspired approaches (i.e. Petryna and Kleinman 2006; Wailoo *et al.* 2010) For example, analysis of knowledge about, access to and use of antiretroviral therapies in Uganda articulates how social relations and distinctions are embedded in the social meanings of medicines, as well as how the medicines enable and articulate the doing of family relationships (Whyte *et al.* 2006, 260), articulations we see resonances of in our material on Viagra. Just as Applbaum (2006) shows in his study of antidepressants in the Japanese market, and with Lakoff's work on antidepressant use in Argentina (Lakoff 2006, 133), our work shows how the market, medical profession and regulatory actors all struggle to define disease and patient groups, and to influence each other in the process. As Lakoff writes, 'the mutual imbrication of science, regulation and business in the circulation of pharmaceuticals is best seen not as a contamination of pure science but rather as part of a distinctive and emergent regime for authorizing knowledge claims and expert action' (Lakoff 2006, 111–12). We draw inspiration from this approach in our analysis of relationships enabled by pharmaceuticals, as well, and with an eye to our own culture, but we challenge the tendency in this body of research to see *global* as a euphemism for West versus the Rest (Löwy 2010; Stockel 2010; and Lindén 2013 are exceptions to this). We assert that it is also interesting and valuable to explore relationships between the local and the global in a developed, Western/Northern, non-US context.

Pharmaceuticals in Sweden

Medical care available in Sweden can be characterized as technically advanced, 'scientifically grounded', evidence-based medicine soundly positioned in the Western/Northern medical knowledge paradigm. This knowledge paradigm is based on the idea that universal medical facts about the body and health exist, and that these should not be dependent on cultural context. Medical facts should travel unhindered across geographical borders. It is this assumption that makes the global reach of pharmaceuticals (and other medical responses to health and illness) possible at the theoretical level. It is also this assumption that allows the global analysis of pharmaceuticals to assume that the West/North is one unit of analysis.

In our close reading of pharmaceuticals in Sweden, however, we problematize this assumption by showing the uniqueness of the Swedish case, and demonstrating that Western/Northern medicine is not a useful analytical category. Western/Northern is actually a trope that hides a great deal of diversity, even beyond the obvious difficulties of placing countries like Japan and Australia in this nominally geographical category (see Abraham 2011, 727). The nation states that would fit into it are a heterogeneous group which responds to global pharma in unique ways. This is an important point to remember in social science and cultural studies work on the pharmaceutical industry and the medical practices it engenders.

Living in an oft-cited example of socialist medicine, Swedish citizens have access to state-subsidized and state-delivered medical care at very little out-of-pocket cost. Funded by the tax system, the Swedish health care structures are based on the idea that everyone should have equal access to the same high quality of care. This is a concept and a system which is firmly ideological and politically linked to the history of socialist rule in Sweden during most of the twentieth century (Shenkin 1973). While the Swedish health care system has not been immune to privatization and neo-liberal impulses during the past decades (see Johansson Krafve 2015), it still remains a system which attempts to provide close-to-free health care for close-to-everyone. This understanding of health care includes heavily subsidized pharmaceutical treatments.

Because the Swedish state subsidizes pharmaceutical costs for all drugs approved within the scheme with a very minimal individual co-pay, our study presents a context in which the individual's theoretical ability to pay is of little interest. We argue that in Sweden, global pharma is confronted with a very regulated market populated by hyper-individualized patients who are also comfortable with a paternalistic welfare state that has long been responsible for giving them their drugs for almost free, as opposed to the privatized and decentralized health care systems in which states are losing (or have never really had) control of pharmaceutical use (see Petryna and Kleinman 2006). Individuals in Sweden are not familiar with the idea that they should pay for their pharmaceuticals at the point of purchase, but are concerned about the collective costs of pharmaceuticals to their tax bill, even as they demand access to treatment.

This setting problematizes discussions in the extant literature which centre on individuals' willingness (and ability) to pay. The development of some pharmaceutical therapies (for erectile dysfunction, male pattern baldness or wrinkles, for example) and not others (malaria is a commonly cited one), and the growth of pharmaceutical treatments labelled *lifestyle drugs*, is testament to the underlying market mechanisms which encourage drug companies to target markets (conceived of as groups of individuals with similar medical and/or pharmaceutical needs) which are capable and willing to pay for their products. 'As drug costs escalate and access becomes hyperindividualized, pharmaceuticals markets generate new social distinctions based on the individual's ability to pay' (Petryna and Kleinman 2006, 7). This common assertion is to some extent an oversimplification. Our book shows with specific empirical studies how this is a more complicated process of market subdivision and creation within well-regulated markets and distribution channels. Specifically, our work provides an example of what happens in pharmaceutical marketing and distribution practices when the tension between cost to the individual meets the Swedish solidarity principle and idea that health care is a general public good. We highlight the tensions in this concept of 'hyperindividualized' pharmaceutical consumption, teasing out how state structures and local and temporal medical consensus can influence access to and use of brand name pharmaceuticals.

Two aspects of the Swedish case are particularly relevant to the glocal relationships of pharmaceuticals: 1) there is a ban on DTC advertising on prescription medicine (with the exception of vaccines), yet the industry seems to sidestep this ban with little reprimand; and 2) the state pays for the majority of the prescription costs for the population. The first has allowed us to analyze 'Patient Information' websites about erectile dysfunction and the localization elements they incorporate. The second has created a very interesting economic context within which doctors debate the use of pharmaceuticals in relation to other costs, the state takes interest in limiting pharmaceutical use, and the judicial system tests these decisions, at the same time as the state has developed industry regulations in close collaboration with commercial interests.

Abraham has pointed out that pharmaceuticalization is occurring even in countries which have a DTC advertising ban on prescription pharmaceuticals, suggesting that we need to look at shifts in regulatory ideology or policy to explain pharmaceuticalization, not just commercial forces (Abraham 2010, 606). While this is certainly true, we would assert that analysis of DTC advertising may also need to be expanded to the actual practices pharmaceutical companies employ, not only the legal frameworks they work within. Sweden has a ban on DTC advertising, like the rest of Europe, but there may be reason to suspect that this ban is only partially functional. The industry-supported information pages about diseases sometimes shamelessly propose the use of pharmaceutical solutions. At times, media reports about new drugs read like industry press releases. When Viagra arrived it was advertised on full-sized posters at bus stops in southern Sweden, despite the ban. And, as research has shown, in Sweden (as in the United Kingdom) there seems to be widespread disregard for the regulations restricting DTC advertisement, and little bite to the regulatory bodies which are supposed to police it (Zetterqvist and Mulinari 2013; Zetterqvist *et al.* 2015). Thus, in the European context, the legality of DTC advertising is not necessarily a sufficiently well-formulated research parameter.

Pharmaceuticalization and the interplay of pharmaceuticals and state regulatory bodies has a long tradition in Sweden, which began regulating approval and marketing of pharmaceuticals in 1934 (Abraham and Lewis 2000, 55), but its form, and that of regulatory systems in the West/North in general, has changed significantly over the past decades. The current state of today's regulatory framework for pharmaceuticals, developed under neo-liberalism, shows how regulatory bodies have been refashioned to facilitate drug development, rather than protect the public, and in particular how these regulatory bodies are co-opted to serve the industry's will rather than the public's need (Brody 2007; Abraham and Ballinger 2012). In Sweden, this has seen the creation of the Medical Products Agency in 1990, which was funded entirely by industry fees and was supposed to accelerate drug approval times (Abraham and Ballinger 2012, 448). As Abraham and Ballinger note, the pattern of establishing a regulatory body to improve approval processes for industry also occurred in the United Kingdom and in Germany during the 1980s and 1990s, which then influenced the EU supranational drug regulatory system with their neo-liberal approach (Abraham and Ballinger 2012, 449; Junker 2014).

Much academic critique of the regulatory system looks at the regulatory bodies that approve pharmaceuticals before they are made available to the public. The work we present in Part 1, however, particularly in Chapter 2, examines a less commonly discussed regulatory actor – the legal system and court decisions on the appropriate use and funding of drugs. Here the Swedish case is very different from that of the United States, as the state pays for prescription drugs and the use and cost of drugs are thereby regulated by a separate administrative body (the Dental and Pharmaceutical Benefits Agency, previously the Pharmaceutical Benefits Board), whose decisions can be appealed through the court system (see Sjögren 2006). This has traditionally not been a course of action (Abraham and Lewis 2000, 71), but the legal battles over subsidizing Viagra marked a change in the regulatory praxis.

Outline of this book

The Swedish case shows how a highly developed nation, which provides universal health care, including universal access to prescription medicine, responds to and shapes the pharmaceutical solutions that a global market presents through the health care system. The existence of a single, tax-based payer for pharmaceuticals can change the faces (in the STS spirit, we would argue this changes the very products themselves) of the pharmaceutical options available to the public. As the following chapters will show, a global blockbuster drug like Viagra becomes a different product in Sweden than Viagra in the United States, and the users of Viagra are glocalized, too.

This book is divided into three parts. In Part 1, we consider policy and bureaucratic responses to the introduction of new pharmaceuticals, in particular Viagra and the possibility of pharmacogenomics. The work here identifies certain arguments which appear to direct the response: solidarity; provision to those in need; how need is determined; and how the pharmaceutical technologies can actually assist or even replace medical doctors in the determination of need. Close reading of the debates surrounding these products shows how a system founded on the principles of solidarity and equal access to health care, including pharmaceuticals, can respond to the profit-driven industry which is providing these products to the state. Part 1 begs questions about how solidarity, citizen rights and biological rights are related, and how they are created in relationship with each other and with pharmaceuticals.

In Part 2, we analyze the medical discourses that surround the introduction of new pharmaceuticals. The first chapter looks at Viagra and how it has influenced the medical understandings of impotence and erectile dysfunction in Sweden. It shows how the presence of an international drug can have implications for medical terminology and the colloquial use of words to describe a social and medical problem, even in a small, linguistically bounded community like Sweden (with approximately nine million speakers). Chapter 5 traces debates around the introduction of alpha-blockers for benign prostate hyperplasia to the Swedish health care market and the shift in treatment methods they implied for an already medicalized condition. Together, these chapters present local examples of how the pharmaceutical products redefine existing health problems as issues with pharmaceutical solutions and how their presence frames the medical community's responses. Impotence shifts from being a condition treated with sex and couple's therapy to a condition for which one takes a pill. Lower urinary tract symptoms for older men move from being treated with surgery to being treated with a medication. Interestingly, this shift is nearly complete in the Viagra case, but is, fifteen years later, still being contested in the case of alpha-blockers.

Part 3 articulates subject positions for pharmaceutical consumers which are created in commercial discourses in Sweden. Specifically, we examine the advertising, disguised as web-based disease informational pages, for Viagra. By thinking through our cases within a theoretical framework of pharmaceuticalization, we see that pharmaceuticals are creating new subject positions around the drugs. Chapter 6 examines the construction and enrolment of (consumer) subjects which are not directly consuming the pill. Here we see how the commercial Viagra discourse produces and enrols the man's partner and his doctor in the production of the Swedish Viagra man. This discourse also directs the relationships the man develops and maintains with his partner and his doctor, and tries to approach the partner and doctor to help them maintain Viagra-mediated relationships with the consuming Swedish Viagra man. Chapter 7 then discusses the creation of the Swedish Viagra man and the particular characteristics assigned to him. It presents an analysis of the culturally specific aspects of Swedish masculinity which Pfizer (or at least its marketing departments and agencies) deemed strong and stable enough to be associated with a product which addresses an image of failed masculinity.

Chapter 8 concludes this volume by returning to the multiplicity of aspects that the term *pharmaceuticalization* contains. Using the literary trope of the Swedish Viagra man, we discuss how the local and the global interact in the Swedish context.

Glocal pharma

The changes in governance practices to reflect pharmaceuticals' presence, the redefinition of health problems as sites of pharmaceutical treatment and the creation of new techno-social identities around drugs are general aspects of pharmaceuticalization apparent in the Swedish case material we present in this book. However, they are also aspects of the local, specific to the Swedish context, which are important to analyze and integrate into a concept of pharmaceuticalization because they show nodes in the pharmaceutical network which are receptive to influence by local specificities. The results of these local influences are what we refer to as the 'glocal of pharmaceuticalization', the local specificities which appear in the discourses embedding global pharmaceutical products and practices in local markets. When local responses to global pharma are enacted in Sweden, the local pushes back.

Persistent traces of the local can be interpreted in a couple of different ways. One could see the process of pharmaceuticalization as an irresistible, all-consuming process, and these local specificities can point to weaknesses in the process. Our observations could be interpreted as aspects of pharmaceuticals where they are not quite strong enough to resist and redirect the local context to their will. Or, these nodes of difference could be seen as examples of where the pharmaceutical discourse is flexible enough to consume and adapt to the local context, where it shows its strength through a colonizing, but not neutralizing practice of meeting local cultures. As Williams and colleagues note, 'there are important sources of resistance to the expansion of pharmaceutical markets from the media, government, medicine, patients and diverse publics thereby making de-pharmaceuticalization a possibility in principle, if infrequent in practice' (Williams *et al.* 2011a, 722). Perhaps our examples of the glocal response to subsidizing Viagra in Sweden in Chapter 2 can indicate that this is more than mere optimism. Resistance is possible. But our analysis of the information sites for Viagra treatments and the medical discourse around Viagra and alpha-blockers in Sweden are harder to read as support for this optimism.

In drawing conclusions about the glocal of pharmaceuticalization, it is useful to ask how a drug's presence has altered the concept of a disease and its treatment, who suffers from it, and how to cure it, in the local context and internationally. This book shows how drugs interact with stereotypical imaginaries of a patient, and include markers of class, race and sexuality. Drugs can influence laws and policies to regulate the practices of both doctors and patients. Yet it is not the chemical compound that prescribes behaviours or identities, it is the network of decision makers, commercial actors, medical experts and consumers who attach the drug to specific demands, images and expectations to influence the behaviours of groups they are trying to govern, cajole or cure. And because actors in different countries have different cultural starting points and are working within different institutional frameworks, how they use a pharmaceutical varies.

By looking at the pharmaceutical nexus and its actors, we can see that a global drug does more than fix the biomedical body's problems. As the following chapters will show, the mere existence of a pharmaceutical product impacts medical knowledge and discourses, reinforces and even constructs cultural ideas and identities, changes the practices of experts and laypeople, and changes policy. But local circumstances also influence how drugs are presented and prescribed and what they are allowed to be. Together, the global and local aspects of the pharmaceutical nexus create *glocal* pharma.

Part 1

Changes in forms of governance

2 Governing by drugs

Conniving patients, beguiled doctors and disciplining drugs[1]

Ebba Sjögren and Ericka Johnson

In April 2001, the Swedish government decided to immediately remove Viagra from the public pharmaceutical reimbursement system (Swedish Book of Statutes 2001, 140). All patients who still wanted their use of these pharmaceuticals to be subsidized were henceforth required to submit individual applications for subsidy to the government itself.

This highly publicized and much-debated decision marked a clear break with the established practice whereby prescription drugs that were granted marketing approval were consistently included in the public pharmaceutical benefits scheme. Under this scheme, patients prescribed subsidized drugs paid only a portion of their direct cost. Following the government's decision, Viagra was still available for purchase in pharmacies by those holding prescriptions, but the patients were now to assume the cost.

The decision to exclude Viagra from the benefits scheme was made in a setting of long debate concerning the rising costs for health care in general, the growing public expenditure on pharmaceuticals in particular, and a concern that a blockbuster drug like Viagra would put undue pressure on the public purse.[2] Yet having the government decide on the subsidization of Viagra on a case-by-case basis was as extraordinary as it sounds. Prior to this, decisions were made on an aggregate level, and this change is an example of the first aspect of pharmaceuticalization we will be discussing, when drugs change the form of governance (Williams *et al.* 2011a). Because of Viagra (and concerns about pharmaceutical costs in general at the time), case-by-case decision practice was first applied and then a new governmental agency was instituted with the responsibility for deciding which pharmaceuticals to subsidize: the Pharmaceutical Benefits Board (here called the TLV to reflect its current name, the Dental and Pharmaceutical Benefits Agency).[3] This new government agency changed the configuration of commercial, regulatory and public interests at the pharmaceutical nexus in Sweden, and led to a series of court cases questioning the TLV's decisions, which we will examine in this chapter. That the decision to deny Viagra from the public pharmaceutical benefits scheme was appealed through the courts is particularly interesting because, while this option had existed in Sweden for some time, it was rarely employed (Abraham and Lewis 2000, 71). The Viagra cases marked a new way of using the courts in the regulation of pharmaceutical policy, but did so within a changed bureaucratic landscape that had a new regulatory body and was grappling with how to define disease, with questions of trust, and with the involvement of patient groups and commercial actors.

Many Western welfare states have, in recent decades, faced the question of how to set boundaries for public fiscal responsibility for health care services. One recurrent solution has been to create central health care assessment organizations tasked with evaluating the appropriateness of undertaking and publicly funding particular treatment methods. The importance of using scientific facts as a decision-making tool in these organizations is typically emphasized (Jost 2005) and has been explored and criticized by social scientists (Pope 2003; Timmermans and Berg 2003, Gray and Harrison 2004; May *et al.* 2006). But whatever the shortcomings of, for example, evidence-based medicine and clinical trials, the organized collection, evaluation, codification and distribution of evidence about treatment effects is still conceived of as a means to achieve a more fair and effective prioritization of limited resources (cf. Cuyler and Newhouse 2000; Mitton and Donaldson 2004). In response to the conceptualization of an evidence-based prioritization imperative, state bodies have been constructed and tasked with the job of turning scientific facts into public policy. The TLV, which was formally launched in October 2002, is an example of such an organization.

By law, the decision-making board of the TLV is instructed to approve subsidy for a drug when: 'the cost of using the pharmaceutical . . . is *reasonable from medical, humanitarian and socio-economic perspectives*' (Swedish Book of Statutes 2002, 160, Section 15; authors' emphasis added). The TLV is further instructed to take into consideration the three principles of priority-setting that Parliament approved in 1997, namely: *equal human value*, meaning all people have an equal right to life and health, *need solidarity*, that those with greatest need of treatment have priority over those with lesser need and *cost-effectiveness*, that the benefit of treatment must be reasonable in relation to its cost (Socialutskottet 1997).[4]

The subsidization status of Viagra was one of the first cases the TLV decided. After a period of deliberation, the TLV decided to exclude Viagra entirely from the Swedish pharmaceutical benefits scheme on 26 March 2003. The marketing company, Pfizer AB, soon appealed the TLV's decision. A series of court battles ensued, ending with a decision by the Swedish Supreme Administrative Court on 14 March 2008. In its ruling, the court upheld the TLV's decision to exclude Viagra from the pharmaceutical benefits scheme in Sweden. Prior to this, two lower courts had overturned the TLV's decision and approved restricted subsidy for Viagra when treating specific categories of patients, which were deemed to fulfil the legal criteria for subsidy. Still today, Viagra is not eligible for use with public subsidy. As the Swedish Supreme Administrative Court took this decision, there is no further legal recourse for appeal of the case. However, the option remains for the pharmaceutical marketing company to submit a new application for subsidy if and when substantively new developments open for the possibility of a different outcome.

In this chapter, we will place the argumentation in the TLV's decision justification documents and the various court rulings in a discussion of trust in regulatory bodies and expert practices by looking at how the TLV and the courts conceive of patients, doctors and subsidized pharmaceuticals. In particular, we will focus on how patients, doctors and drugs are framed within the subsidy discourse surrounding Viagra and how drugs themselves are used as diagnostic tools and to enforce subsidy decisions. We will argue that, notwithstanding the legal criteria for approving subsidy, the ultimate denial of subsidy in the Viagra case relied on a construction of imagined behaviours and roles for patients, doctors and drugs as recipients and enforcers of subsidy decisions. A comparison of the various decision justifications points to a concern for patient misuse of the subsidy, difficulties for doctors to deny subsidy and an organizational concern for bracket creep, all of which were thought to potentially lead to unreasonably high public spending on Viagra. In our discussion we problematize some of the assumptions on which the framing of actors is based.

While the particular circumstances of the Viagra case are specific to Sweden, we see the TLV and its work as an example of a strengthened emphasis on mechanical objectivity and bureaucratic compliance in the management and control of health care services, issues which are relevant in other contexts, as well. This development – while by no means unidirectional – is nonetheless relevant to consider in light of the many rules, standards and decisions which target the contents of medical practice from a distance (Timmermans and Berg 2003; Lagrelius and Sjögren 2004). We see that the example of Viagra raises a number of pertinent practical and theoretical concerns linked to the emergence of techno-social identities. We also want to emphasize the way the pharmaceuticals themselves, especially the materiality of their delivery technologies, were enrolled in the regulatory decisions and that these actors shaped the local regulatory practices.

Empirical material

The following account focuses on how the TLV justified its decision to deny subsidy for Viagra use, and how these justifications were judged. Our material derives from: the TLV's original decision justification document, 26 March 2003 (Pharmaceutical Benefits Board 2003a); the argumentation set out in court rulings made by the Stockholm Lower Administrative Court in June 2004 (Länsrätten 2004a); the argumentation set out in court rulings made by the Stockholm Administrative Appellant Court in April 2005 (Kammarrätten in Stockholm 2005a); the argumentation set out in court rulings made by the Supreme Administrative Court in March 2008 (Regeringsrätten 2008 a, b, c).

We will also consider the contents of the Pharmaceutical Benefit Board's decision justification documents concerning two other pharmaceutical-based treatments of erectile dysfunction for which the TLV approved subsidy: Caverject and Bondil. The TLV's decisions in these two cases were referenced in several court proceedings, thereby making them empirically relevant for our analysis.

Of note is that the decisions these documents present were made by collectives, and they were not unanimous decisions. Dissenting members of the TLV's decision-making board and the Supreme Administrative Court have stated their grounds for disagreeing with the final outcome of particular decision-making processes in writing.

The Pharmaceutical Benefits Board, the law and Viagra

With the creation of the TLV, by law, the decision about whether to subsidize a pharmaceutical was to be determined by characteristics of its use.[5] Regardless of which conclusion the TLV reaches as regards a pharmaceutical's subsidization status, it must publicly justify this outcome in a so-called decision justification document. This document has an important legal status. It is the basis for any appeal of the TLV's decision (Swedish Book of Statutes 2002, Section 26, 160). Various procedural requirements are set out for the appeals process. Notably, the law restricts the right of appealing the decision concerning a particular drug to the company marketing that pharmaceutical. The appeal must be submitted within a strict time frame. The legislation also sets out that it is the Stockholm County Administrative Court (henceforth 'the Lower Court') which will rule on an appeal, followed by the Administrative Court of Appeal in Stockholm (henceforth 'the Appellant Court') and the Supreme Administrative Court ('the Supreme Court').

In comparison to the fairly detailed procedural regulation of the appeals process, the substantive basis for judicial review of the Pharmaceutical Benefits Board's decision-making is less clear-cut. The legislation does not specify in detail what it means for a pharmaceutical to have a 'reasonable' cost of use. Some clarification is provided in the legislative bill (New Pharmaceutical Benefits Bill 2001). However, this document also includes repeated references to the need for imprecise instructions for the TLV due to the difficulty of specifying practice for an organization with a new and complicated task. The onus is therefore on the TLV to make decisions that can be justified and judged as being in accordance with the TLV's governing legislation. It is to a consideration of these justifications, and the court's judgements, to which we now turn. These can be briefly summarized as follows:

2003: The TLV denies subsidy for Viagra

In its decision justification document from March 2003, the TLV acknowledges that Viagra may be a reasonable drug to subsidize for patients with severe ED. However, the judgement is that the agency does not have the means for ensuring that subsidy is restricted only to those patients whose treatment needs fulfil the legal criteria for publicly funded pharmaceutical use (Pharmaceutical Benefits Board 2003c, 4); the risk that non-worthy patients would receive subsidized medicine and opening the door for diagnostic bracket creep is such that all use is denied subsidy.

2004: The Lower Court approves restricted subsidy to 'reasonable' patients with certain medical conditions or a treating specialist

In 2004, the Lower Court rules to reverse the TLV's denial of subsidy, and approves subsidy with restrictions to patients with certain medical conditions such as diabetes or cardiovascular diseases, or who were prescribed the drugs by a urologist. Unlike the TLV, the Lower Court concludes that the scientific studies the pharmaceutical companies submitted show the pharmaceutical to be generally cost-effective, and therefore reasonable. In contrast to the TLV, the Lower Court also judges that the two other pharmaceutical-based treatments of male impotence – Caverject and Bondil – are relevant comparisons. Viagra (and Cialis and Levitra) was deemed cost-effective in comparison to Caverject and Bondil, which had been approved for subsidy in the intervening year between the TLV's decision on Viagra and the Lower Court's decision (see also Länsrätten in Stockholm 2004b; 2004c, 13, 25).

The TLV immediately appealed this decision. While the appeal was pending, Viagra (and Cialis and Levitra) was not subsidized.

2005: The Appellant Court approves restricted subsidy on different grounds: specialists to make appropriate diagnosis of 'reasonable' patients

The Appellant Court did not uphold the TLV's subsequent appeal of the Lower Court's ruling. However, the Appellant Court *did* change the definition of the restrictions for approved subsidy. In the Appellant Court's ruling, Viagra was granted restricted subsidy for: 'patients with the [medical condition] severe erectile dysfunction, regardless of underlying illness. Initial prescription [is] to be made by a physician with specialist competence in urology' (Kammarrätten in Stockholm 2005, 18).

In contrast to the Lower Court's conclusion, the Appellant Court agreed with the TLV's initial conclusion that the cited clinical studies showed that only patients with severe male impotence were reasonable to treat. However, the Appellant Court agreed with the Lower Court's argument that medical practitioners could dependably identify patients who were 'reasonable' to subsidize. Yet the diagnosis-based restriction the Lower Court set was not deemed to correctly identify those patients who should receive subsidized treatments. Rather, the Appellant Court argued that restricting subsidy to initial prescription by a medical specialist on male reproductive organs (urologist) was a (more) dependable way of determining 'reasonable' patients.

The TLV also immediately appealed this decision. It would take three years for the Supreme Court to make its decision in the case.

2008: The Supreme Court denies all subsidy

Based on the existence of Bondil and Caverject, the uncertainty of a 'severe ED' diagnosis, the imagined behaviours of patients and doctors and the risk for diagnostic bracket creep, the Supreme Court denied all subsidy of Viagra (and Cialis and Levitra) in 2008. We will now discuss this decision.

Discussion: conniving patients, beguiled doctors and disciplining drugs

Diagnostic dilemmas: identifying the right patients to treat with subsidized drugs

In the final Supreme Court decision that Viagra would not be subsidized, the TLV argued it would be impossible to limit the subsidization of Viagra to appropriately needy and deserving patients, and therefore the drug should not be subsidized at all. As the TLV puts forward in its argument:

> Doctors will rely upon the patient's responses and understandings [to questions about their ED], which in practice means that it is impossible for the individual doctor to deny the patient a subsidized prescription if the patient demands it. Likewise, the patient can nearly always be expected to want to have the medication subsidized.
>
> (Regeringsrätten 2008a, 3)

The implication is that all, or at least a significant number of, patients with mild ED – those not considered deserving of the subsidy – could be expected to connive and wile their way into a diagnosis of severe ED, beguiling their doctors into making this diagnosis and thereby receiving subsidized Viagra instead of paying for it themselves.

Why are patients and doctors represented this way? Why does the TLV (and apparently the Supreme Court, which agreed to its arguments) distrust patients and declare doctors incapable of withstanding a patient's wishes in the clinical setting, implying that the layperson/expert relationship has broken down?[6] Other research has shown this dynamic does occur in the patient/doctor meeting (cf. Hirschauer 1998, 16; Timmermans and Berg 2003, 121; Friberg 2006). And empowered, knowledgeable patients who make demands on their health care providers exist, and are cultivated by both patient groups and care providers. But one would assume the belief still exists that doctors are capable of objectively diagnosing disease. Yet, actually, the (in)ability of doctors to assess the severity of ED was already questioned and debated in the original TLV decision document, although three board members disagreed with this, stating:

> The only ones who can determine if a patient has severe ED are the patient, his partner, and his doctor. This type of decision occurs daily and repeatedly for all sorts of illnesses in a doctor's day-to-day practice, with varying degrees of certainty. To determine ED can hardly be more difficult than to determine if a patient is suffering from depression, pain or any other state for which the doctor must primarily rely on information from the patient.
>
> (Pharmaceutical Benefits Board 2003c, 5)

But they were in the minority. The idea of conniving patients and beguiled doctors continued to appear and became one of the important framing arguments in the Supreme Court decision. We suggest that when it appears in the arguments put forward to the Supreme Court, the construction of conniving patients and beguiled doctors is relating and responding to earlier arguments about the reasonableness of Viagra and prior decisions to subsidize other medical treatments of ED.

It is important to keep in mind that throughout the debate about subsidies, it was generally agreed that Viagra was a 'reasonable' drug to subsidize for severe ED.[7] The Supreme Court, for example, stated that it was 'uncontested that medical treatment of severe ED is to be considered urgent and that treatment with Viagra in these cases is cost-effective' (Regeringsrätten 2008a, 9). And in the original decision justification document, the TLV formulated its views on the 'reasonableness' of treating patients with severe ED as follows:

> [T]he diagnosis [of] ED is so wide that one can include everything from complete inability [to achieve an erection] to the occasional inability [to achieve an erection]. The Board can therefore determine that the degree of suffering for all individuals who are affected by ED is not so great that it can dictate that the group as a whole has a large need of care in relationship to many other patient groups. In addition, a gradual reduction in erectile ability is a natural part of aging. According to the Board's understanding, it can hardly be the general public's (*allmännas*) task to ensure that a person can live with the same functionality for the entire life. . . . The Board has considered if it would be possible to adopt a qualified decision which would allow Viagra to be subsidized only for those who suffer from severe ED, which can be more appropriate to treat medically and where one can assume that the medicine would be cost-effective. The Board cannot, however, find appropriate restrictions which would make it possible in this case to limit the subsidy to only those who have a socioeconomically reasonable need of subsidized treatment.
> (Pharmaceutical Benefits Board 2003c, 4)

Thus, already in the original decision document the TLV admits it may be reasonable to subsidize Viagra for patients with severe ED, but that existing medical practice is not capable of or trusted enough to provide diagnoses that meet the level of certainty that the TLV as a bureaucratic institution demands, that is to distinguish without a doubt which patients have mild ED and which have severe ED. The problem was, for the TLV and the Supreme Court, there was no reliable way to determine if a patient suffered from severe or merely mild ED.

Debates over diagnostic tools: questionnaires, urologists and patients' accounts

A tool exists for measuring ED: the International Index of Erectile Function (IIEF). However, in the various decision-making processes involving the subsidization status of Viagra disagreement recurred about its ability to actually determine the severity of ED. According to the TLV in the court documents, this questionnaire was developed for other (research) purposes and is only really used as a support or crutch in the patient meeting, and not as a diagnostic instrument (Regeringsrätten 2008a, 3). The TLV's position, as described in the Supreme Court ruling, is that: 'the questionnaire provides no guarantee that the information provided by the questions is a mirror of reality' (Regeringsrätten 2008a, 3). Furthermore, the TLV does not see the IIEF as a necessary diagnostic tool because doctors can diagnose their patients' ED without it. Yet when making this diagnosis, doctors will have to rely on patients' information and experiences, rather than a scientific tool. Therefore, the TLV claims that doctors are powerless to deny the truth of patients' stories, thus making it impossible to deny the patients subsidized Viagra if the patients demand it (presumably by telling doctors they have severe ED) (Regeringsrätten 2008a, 3).

Expert testimony, particularly in the Lower Court, supported the claim that the IIEF *was* primarily used as a conversational aid, not a diagnostic tool, and that doctors *did* have to rely on conversations with patients to determine the severity of the ED. Like in the dissenting opinion of the original decision document, arguments were put forth through the entire debate that this type of diagnosis is something doctors are qualified to do, and do in their daily practice with many other diseases. However, these arguments did not provide sufficient reassurance to the TLV or the Supreme Court that the diagnosis of severe ED was being made on certain, scientific grounds.

The difficulty of diagnosing severe ED also carried with it another problem for the TLV. According to the Supreme Court documents, because it was impossible to identify objectively, scientifically and with certainty the group of patients who should be covered, it would also be impossible to develop bureaucratic structures which could check that the subsidy was correctly applied. Following on from this was a series of arguments against the use of specialist doctors to regulate the prescription of Viagra to those with severe ED, which the Appellant Court decision had dictated. However, one of the biggest problems with relying on specialists to diagnose severe ED was an uneven distribution of specialists in the country, which meant many people would not have access to a specialist. If patients were forced to rely on visiting a specialist for the prescription of the drug, those patients living in areas without access to them would be discriminated against by the health care system, which would go against the principle of equal access to health care guaranteed by law (Swedish Book of Statutes 1982, 763). Additionally, the TLV argued that restricting prescription rights to specialist doctors could only be motivated for control reasons, not medical reasons, which would not lead to an optimal use of resources within the health care system (Regeringsrätten 2008a, 3–4).

Likewise, when discussing the use of specialist doctors the TLV asserted that because the disease of ED is flexible and patients' experience of it variable, both over time and from patient to patient, it is not a sufficiently stable condition to warrant one initial truth-determining moment with a specialist. An initial prescription by a specialist would, therefore, not guarantee that the medicine would only be used for the most severe cases over an extended period of time (Regeringsrätten 2008a, 4). A man with severe ED at one appointment may get better and have mild ED later. Thus there was no trusting that even a specialist could apply the criteria for subsidizing the medication appropriately. However, we feel that the most interesting element in the debate is the existence of and subsidy for Bondil and Caverject.

Pharmaceuticals as alternative tools for resolving problems of diagnosis

The TLV granted subsidy for Bondil and Caverject a few months after the agency denied subsidy for Viagra (Pharmaceutical Benefits Board 2003d; 2003e). Bondil is a medication in 'dissolvable stick' form inserted into the urethra. It can be administered by the man himself, after initial training by a medical professional, and produces an erection after about ten minutes. Caverject is injected directly into the erectile tissue of the penis. It is also possible for the man to inject himself with Caverject, although training with a medical professional is also recommended. Both Caverject and Bondil were, at the time, more expensive than Viagra, although they now cost about the same per dose. So, as Pfizer argued in the court cases (and as was also noted in the dissenting opinions in both the original Caverject and Bondil decision documents; Pharmaceutical Benefits Board 2003d; 2003e), Viagra was more cost-effective than Caverject and Bondil – all else being equal (Länsrätten in Stockholm 2004, 9; Kammarrätten in Stockholm 2005, 16). As previously noted, whether all else *was* equal was very hotly contested. For both the TLV and the Supreme Court, it was important for the decision to deny subsidy for Viagra that neither Caverject nor Bondil was particularly easy or pleasant to use. Notably, the Supreme Court justified its decision to uphold the TLV's decision to deny subsidy for Viagra since:

> It is true that the drugs Caverject and Bondil are subsidized. In the decision regarding these two substances, however, it was assumed that because of the methods of use, they will primarily be used to treat patients who suffer from the most severe forms of ED. The general subvention decision is, therefore, in practice limited to only those cases of ED for which would also be reasonable to subsidize Viagra. The subsidy for Caverject and Bondil can therefore not be used as an argument that Viagra should also be granted general subsidy.
>
> (Regeringsrätten 2008a, 8)

Also in the Lower and Appellant Court rulings it was implied, and sometimes stated outright, that a patient with mild ED might be tempted to try Viagra, but he would not be tempted to try injecting or inserting medicine directly into his penis. Repeatedly in the documents it is claimed that Bondil and Caverject have built-in mechanisms that prevent their 'misuse' or at least their 'mis-subsidization' by patients suffering from only mild ED, and the TLV can thus claim that it is providing a subsidized treatment for patients who suffer from severe ED, which will not be misused (Länsrätten in Stockholm 2004, 9). Thus, one could assert that when the TLV argues before the Supreme Court that Viagra should not be subsidized, it is really saying that there is no sufficiently reliable medical tool in clinical practice to determine the severity of ED which would fulfil the objectivity demands of the bureaucratic subsidy system. According to the TLV's arguments, patients can be expected to exaggerate the severity of their problem in order to receive (desirable) subsidized drugs. Doctors will probably be beguiled or bullied into agreeing with the patients. And the diagnostic questionnaire the industry and certain medical practitioners suggest for determining severity is not a reliable tool, either. Instead, in the case of ED, the bureaucracy that regulates subsidies relies on the physical characteristics of two other medicines to discipline the patients and determine the severity of disease. Bondil and Caverject become 'bitter pills' that only a sufficiently ill person could reasonably be expected to swallow. Thus, their use by a given patient reifies a diagnosis of severe ED.

Reliance on the physical characteristics of a technology (pharmaceutical) to prevent misdiagnosis and mis-subsidizing of drugs against ED is important because it is thought to reduce the risk of diagnostic bracket creep, that is to limit the risk that the drug will be prescribed for a larger group of symptoms or for less severe symptoms that were previously untreated. There are other examples where the TLV pinned its hopes on a technology that might serve to remove ambiguity related to the correct diagnosis of 'treatable' patients, such as the organization's review of pharmaceuticals for the treatment of stomach acid–related disorders (Pharmaceutical Benefits Board 2003b; see also Sjögren 2006).

The assertion of a risk of diagnostic bracket creep goes back to the argument that a patient is always going to want to have his medication subsidized, even if he knows that he really only has mild ED (or a stomach ache), and will therefore pressure his doctor into agreeing that he actually has severe ED. Since, in this scenario, the patient's description of ED is not to be trusted, alternative methods for creating unambiguous knowledge about the condition must be used. Doctors, in the TLV's ideal world, must be able to rely on scientific diagnostic tools to help them make correct decisions in their clinical practice. But since the available tool (the IIEF) is deemed unreliable, instead the TLV relies on the drugs themselves to do the disciplining work.

Conclusion

The TLV was purposefully created to decide the subsidization status of prescription pharmaceuticals and to take part in shaping the use of public funds for pharmaceutical spending. In this chapter, we have focused on how the TLV and the courts conceived of patients, doctors and subsidized pharmaceuticals when determining the subsidization status of Viagra. Notwithstanding the legal criteria for approving subsidy, we have argued in the previous section that the ultimate denial of subsidy in the Viagra case relied on a construction of imagined behaviours and roles for patients, doctors and drugs as recipients and enforcers of subsidy decisions. A comparison of the various decision justifications points to a suspicion of patient misuse of the subsidy, difficulties for doctors to deny subsidy and an organizational concern for bracket creep, all of which could potentially lead to unreasonably high public spending on Viagra. In this section, we will reflect on the consequences of these observations, against the organizational remit of the TLV and the role of pharmaceuticals in fulfilling the regulatory ambitions of the organization. In particular, we will touch on the use of pharmaceuticals as disciplining technology and a possible differentiation between bureaucratic and treatment compliance.

Use of pharmaceuticals as disciplining technology

The term *disease mongering* is often used for the process by which the existence of a drug (or other form of treatment) is used to create and/or promote the notion of a disease meriting treatment. Marshall (2002; 2006) and Tiefer (2000; 2006) have shown this development using the case of erectile dysfunction and the marketing of Viagra, but other drug–disease pairs have also been connected to disease mongering: the development of SSRI inhibitors and the increased diagnosing of depression (cf. Healy 2004), and lifestyle drugs and diseases like hair loss (Rogaine), wrinkles (Botox) and shyness (beta-blockers) (Elliott 2003; Moynihan and Cassels 2005). In these cases, the existence of a treatment serves as a motivation behind the medicalization of a particular state of being and the definition of a disease.

Studies within science, technology and medicine have examined how medications can be ascribed even stronger ontological roles. For example, in his exploration of bronchodilators, Willems demonstrates how these drugs work within a network of researchers, laboratory assistants and measurement devices to create disease classifications. In this example, the drugs 'define diseases and reorganize the body by creating new identities for it' (Willems 1998, 118). Similar events have been detailed for arteriosclerosis (Mol 2002), liver disease (Law and Singleton 2005) and IUD contraception practices (Dugdale 2000). Medical technologies can be silent and unrecognized actors that take part in producing particular configurations of diseases or patients, as an outcome of the technologies' use in a network of actors. In the present case, however, we understand the TLV's use of Caverject and Bondil as a conscious and explicit deployment of technologies to this purpose.

As described earlier, the TLV deemed Viagra reasonable to subsidize for patients with severe ED. However, the tools necessary to identify and sort patients based on the severity of ED were deemed insufficiently reliable. This highlights that the clinical practice involved in prescribing Viagra is messy. That clinical practice is messy makes it difficult to regulate, difficult to define and certainly difficult to standardize (Berg and Mol 1998; Timmermans and Berg 2003). So when a bureaucratic body such as the TLV is confronted with obvious examples of how that messy clinical practice is going to be difficult to regulate (and difficult to enforce any regulation within), the organization looks for other means of disciplining it. By granting Bondil and Caverject subsidy while denying subsidy for Viagra, the TLV is relying on particular physical characteristics of these two drugs to replace the diagnostic responsibilities and perceived shortcomings of medical doctors in clinical practice.

We suggest that the way that the TLV searches for (and finally finds in the case of Caverject and Bondil) an 'objective' tool to define and diagnose severe ED can be related to the two different types of objectivity explicated by Porter (1995). Porter differentiates between disciplinary objectivity and mechanical objectivity. The former is found in specialist communities and can be characterized by consensus between equals, trust, tacit knowledge and the artful application of insight. It is also associated with a disdain for standards. In many ways, disciplinary objectivity is what the expert witnesses relied on when they claimed throughout the various decision documents analyzed in this chapter that doctors are entirely capable of diagnosing severe ED when meeting patients, with or without the assistance of the IIEF. It is also what the Appellant Court decided to rely on when it ruled that subsidized Viagra should initially be prescribed by urologists.

Mechanical objectivity, on the other hand, replaces trust in experts with mechanical rules, procedures and numbers, and is what the TLV is trying to find when relying on Caverject and Bondil to define severe ED. Porter argues that mechanical objectivity through independently verifiable rules and procedures can be used by an expert community (like the TLV) to create legitimacy. It 'is a way of making decisions without seeming to decide; [it] lends authority to officials who have very little of their own' (Porter 1995, 8). Perhaps it is no surprise, then, that the TLV, which was created only in 2002, would rely on this type of mechanical objectivity. Not only does its young age mean that it needs to create legitimacy for its decision, but also the very fact that the agency is being taken to court over its decisions indicates that the TLV's authority is being questioned. Furthermore, the TLV is looking to intervene in what has historically been an activity (treatment choice) that has constituted an important part of the mandate of a strong professional group (physicians) (cf. Porter 1995, 228). Taken together, this would arguably encourage reliance on mechanical objectivity, rather than the trust and legitimacy of an expert community, and the Supreme Court decision supports the employment of this kind of mechanical objectivity.

Bureaucratic versus treatment compliance

Given how the process of determining Viagra's subsidization status unfolded, there was no move to adopt any kind of more flexible version of objectivity. As a parallel to Porter's *differentiation* between disciplinary and mechanical objectivity, we would posit that the TLV's deployment of Caverject and Bondil is intended to take part in creating circumstances that minimize the risk of non-compliance. But it is non-compliance in a particular manner and mode.

As a consequence of the TLV's formal and delimited task to make knowledge-based decisions about the subsidization status of prescription pharmaceuticals, we see a concern with the bureaucratic compliance to these decisions. This is in contrast with the *general compliance* to the agency's individual decisions within medical practice. This contrasts with what we would loosely term *treatment compliance*, by which we refer to compliance that involves consideration of multiple rules, decisions and principles *in an individual case*. The latter form of compliance is typically inferred in relation to treatment guidelines, for example, where it is common practice to state that the guideline is a standard, which is discretionary to follow, rather than a directive, which must be adhered to (cf. Brunsson and Jacobsson 2000). These two ideas of compliance imply very different versions of what constitutes 'good practice', where the latter is more malleable and ambiguous. It is worth reminding the reader here that the decisions the TLV takes, and its desire for objective diagnostics and disciplining tools, come at a point in time when the Swedish health care and social insurance agencies are under fire for excessively permissive long-term sick leave in what the media presented as unreasonably large segments of the populations, thereby draining the coffers of the social welfare state.

The more 'singular' version of bureaucratic compliance constructs a different scope and means for balancing judgement and distributing responsibility between patient/doctor/TLV and the state than does the idea of treatment compliance. Notably, scholars have argued that regulation, which maintains ambiguity over the conditions for appropriate use, contributes to moving responsibility away from those with the formal power to regulate use (cf. Rappert 2001).

We therefore see certain parallels between how the TLV itself is regulated and evaluated, and how the agency seeks to regulate medical professionals. In the case of the TLV, there are precise procedural requirements for the organization's decision-making process and comparatively loose substantive criteria. Due to the manner and means of oversight – primarily through the requirement for public accounting of the grounds for every decision outcome, and further through appeals – it is the mechanical objectivity of the TLV that is emphasized rather than the expert judgement that the agency is encouraged to use.[8] That the TLV is evaluated for how it makes and justifies decisions could arguably serve to emphasize the organization's procedural, bureaucratic compliance (cf. Power 1997). This could, in turn, shift the responsibility for perceived shortcomings in how boundaries for public fiscal responsibility for pharmaceutical use are drawn to the TLV (and, by extension, individual medical practitioners) – and away from the national policymakers who have given the organization this challenging task.

How the TLV was tasked with regulatory responsibility and how it perceived its role as a regulating body are examples of local, nation state–specific responses to the integration of international pharma within an allegedly culturally neutral, objective and scientific medical knowledge paradigm. While of course, the TLV exists within an international pharmaceutical regulatory framework, especially the EU one, as Abraham and Lewis (2000) explore, it and its decisions are nonetheless indelibly tinted by the cultural aspects of the Swedish medical system. The introduction of a drug like Viagra refracts uniquely within it as the drug and framework encounter each other. A new drug and a new regulatory body led to new regulatory tools and, because of local structures (like the uneven distribution of urologists throughout the country) and the culturally specific ideology of the health care system's framework (with the principle of equal access to health care guaranteed by law), the drug precipitated a debate and decision about subsidy based on local structural and ideological aspects of the Swedish health care system. The glocal of Viagra is inseparable from the local of the TLV and erectile dysfunction. This chapter articulates the construction of a Swedish Viagra coloured by the TLV and value judgements about what ED is within the ideology of the Swedish health care system. This glocal Viagra becomes a drug with uniquely Swedish diagnostic and prescription values, practices and concerns.

Notes

1 An earlier version of this chapter has been published as Sjögren, E. and Johnson, E. (2012). Conniving Patients, Beguiled Doctors and Disciplining Drugs: Justifying the Denial of Subsidy for Viagra Use in Sweden. In Martin Letell, Bengt Larsson and

Håkan Thorn, *Re-engineering the Social? Transformations of the Swedish Welfare State*. Basingstoke: Palgrave, 181–96.

2 For a discussion of this process, see Christensen and Lægreid (2002); Lindbom (2002); Premfors and colleagues (2003).

3 As of 1 September 2008, the TLV broadened its scope of responsibility, which now also includes the evaluation of dental treatments.

4 From the TLV's webpage, www.tlv.se, accessed 5 June 2008. This and all other translations are the authors' own.

5 When the pharmaceutical benefits scheme was first launched, the inclusion of a drug in the scheme was determined by the medical condition(s) it was approved to treat. Medicinalstyrelsen, a precursor to the National Board of Health and Welfare, was responsible for deciding which medical conditions were granted subsidized pharmaceutical treatment. Whether an individual patient's pharmaceutical use was subsidized then depended on the diagnosis set by the treating medical professional. The diagnosis-based system for deciding subsidy was abandoned a few decades later in favour of a product-based system, which was in place at the time of the TLV's creation. The overarching principle of a product-based system is that subsidy is decided by product: either a pharmaceutical is approved for subsidy or it is not. And since the inception of the TLV, a pharmaceutical is not subsidized unless the TLV has reached the decision to approve subsidy. See Sjögren (2006).

6 Our analysis builds in part on the assumption that doctors/experts are not asking for this steering from above. Studies of the emergence of evidence-based medicine (EBM) note that it has its ideological and practical foundations in intra-professional quality improvement efforts (see, for example, Claridge and Fabian 2005; Hult 2006). However, attempts to exercise control of medical treatment choice decisions based on standards of best treatment have since been appropriated by actors and agendas beyond the medical professions, such as administrators, politicians and third party special interests (Pope 2003; Timmermans and Berg 2003).

7 The documents we have seen all seem to agree that at least severe forms of ED are a medical condition worthy of treatment. There were no references to the morality debates that surrounded Viagra when it was introduced, probably because the documents we have analyzed were from 2003 and later, at least five years after the initial introduction of Viagra.

8 Notably, the legislative bill that was submitted to Parliament explicitly states that the precise interpretation of the law is left to the TLV as it 'develops practice' (New Pharmaceutical Benefits Bill 2001, 47).

3 'A few good men' are not enough

Upsetting general categories with specific knowledge when making reimbursement decisions[1]

Ebba Sjögren

Two overarching arguments in this volume are that situating pharmaceuticals in any particular locality recasts the identities and actions of various actors and forges new relationships between health problems and pharmaceutical-based solutions. The other chapters trace various avenues through which ostensibly globally standardized drugs become enmeshed in local discourses and socio-technical arrangements. However, the localization of pharmaceuticals does not automatically give rise to increased pharmaceuticalization. The cases of Viagra and alpha-blockers discussed in Chapters 4 and 5, respectively, highlight differences in the trajectory of pharmaceuticalization when drugs are introduced into areas with varying degrees of medicalization. In the previous chapter, the protracted legal battle over the reimbursement status of Viagra was ultimately resolved by a broadly excluding court ruling which denied all public funding.

This outcome was argued on the basis of structural and ideological aspects of the Swedish health care system, notably including the principle of equal access to health care. Here, I extend the analysis of how pharmaceutical treatment changes forms of governance and I argue that the possibility for making broadly exclusive or inclusive decisions may be strained by the widespread ambition to make pharmaceutical treatment more individualized, notably through technical advancements in the targeting of pharmaceutical-based treatment. To date, such commercially available products are rare. However, their introduction will arguably add to existing challenges with addressing subcategories of users and uses in the regulation of access to pharmaceutical treatment. I use the examples of management of reimbursement for Viagra and other conventional drugs to suggest that a greater precision in delimiting and linking categories of treatable patients and reimbursable drugs can make existing arrangements for defining the boundaries of fiscal responsibility for pharmaceutical use less robust. This nuances the promissory discourse around widespread access to individualized pharmaceutical-based treatment in particular, and the sustained momentum of pharmaceuticalization in general.

In the past decade, detractors have aimed intensified critique against the revolutionary model of biotechnology previously espoused by many researchers, policymakers and representatives of the pharmaceutical industry. Notwithstanding the formative influence of such expectations on the development trajectories of the field (Hedgecoe and Martin 2003), a growing body of research brings into question the linear model of innovation based on observations of an incremental spread of so-called pharmacogenomic technologies 'from bench to bedside' (Hopkins *et al.* 2007). A recurrent conclusion is that '[t]he translation of this science into new technology is far more difficult, costly and time-consuming than many policy-makers believe' (Nightingale and Martin 2004, 564).

While pharmacogenomics has many definitions, a recurrent core claim is that increased knowledge about the human genome and the genetic precursors of disease can contribute to greater certainty of diagnosis and improved effectiveness of treatment. Thus, in addition to generically promoting the continued possibility of drug-based treatment for a growing number of health problems, the pharmacogenomics project seeks both to reconfigure how patients, diseases and treatments are characterized and categorized, and how categories of patients, diseases and treatments are linked. One overarching explanation for the difficulty of developing and implementing pharmacogenomic technologies is that they – like all pharmaceutical-based treatments – must be embedded in existing organizational, professional and financial arrangements. New socio-technological networks emerge as incumbent structures that are reconfigured by the introduction of new technologies and attendant material and discursive practices (Callon 1987; Bijker 1995; Jasanoff 2004). This chapter seeks to contribute to an understanding of how pharmaceuticals shape governance by foregrounding one setting in which such technologies must be situated: decision-making about health care coverage, specifically pharmaceutical reimbursement.

Determining the scope of coverage is a generic concern for both private insurers and health care systems, which operate with public funding. Unsurprisingly, the matter of health care provision, and especially the evaluation of products' cost-effectiveness, has been identified as an important contributing factor to the integration of any new pharmacogenomics product into local health care systems (Hedgecoe 2004, 179–80; Hopkins *et al.* 2006; Gurwitz *et al.* 2009). The use of evidence-based evaluation mechanisms has been seen as an important means of resolving the economic challenges expected to arise from the treatment possibilities more personalized therapies afford (Phillips *et al.* 2004). A dominant research theme has been the development of techniques for analyzing the economic impact of pharmacogenomic technologies. To date these studies have been largely exploratory (for example Flowers and Veenstra 2004; Dervieux and Bala 2006; Payne and Shabaruddin 2010). Relatively few pharmacogenomic technologies have reached the development stage where the matter of coverage is raised. Thus, the actual practices of deciding the scope of health care provision have garnered comparatively little attention from scholars, as compared to the impact of pharmacogenomics on drug development (Lesko and Woodcock 2004; Ginsburg *et al.* 2005; Phillips and Van Bebber 2006; Pendergast 2008) and clinical use (Hedgecoe 2004, 2008; Kirchheiner *et al.* 2005; Lakoff 2006). However, scholars have previously posited challenges with incorporating the results of tools such as cost-benefit analysis into existing regulatory systems. For example, Raj (2002) notes that many existing systems for deciding coverage for so-called orphan drugs generally fail to acknowledge the problem of scarce resources.

With the advent of pharmacogenomics technologies, he argues, these arrangements will have difficulties addressing the likely emergence of a larger number of 'new orphan groups', that is, categories of patients for which it is commercially unattractive to develop tailored therapies. In anticipation of a growing number of pharmacogenomic products that allow for more individually targeted drug-based treatment, a purpose of this chapter is to inquire into the workings of one critical regulatory setting where evaluations of such technologies' cost-effectiveness will be used as part of determining coverage. This is done through a detailed inquiry into the activities of one of the many governmental health care assessment bodies that have been created in Western welfare states over the past decades (Jost 2005).

In studying the Swedish governmental agency tasked with deciding the scope of the public pharmaceutical benefits scheme, I engage with an issue that previous research has identified as pivotal to the development and implementation trajectories of biotechnology in general and pharmacogenomics in particular: the politics of classification (Bowker and Star 1999; Miller and Rose 2008). It is well known that the delineation and management of populations as objects of knowledge and intervention is a political project with significant material impact (Hacking 1999; Foucault 2007, 2008). A growing number of studies highlight the considerable commercial, clinical and ethical stakes that a geneticization of disease classifications (Hedgecoe 2002), and the possibility and practice of patient stratification (Hedgecoe and Martin 2003; Hedgecoe 2004; Reardon 2004; Egalite and Godard 2007; Prainsack 2007), bring to the fore.

This chapter focuses on how categories of 'treatable patients' and 'reimbursable pharmaceutical use' are constructed. Crucially, these categories are interdependent: patients are treatable if they can be linked to a functioning treatment regime. Similarly, a pharmaceutical use is only reimbursable if it treats patients in a medical and economically viable manner. An evaluation of viability takes into consideration various forms of knowledge about pharmaceuticals' medical and economic effects, derived from clinical studies and clinical practice. I will illustrate how this knowledge is articulated at different levels of aggregation and with varying degrees of accuracy, which gives rise to recurrent ambiguity as to how patients and interventions should be characterized and categorized. This ambiguity must be addressed in order to construct stable categories of patients, diseases and drugs that can serve as objects for regulatory intervention. I suggest that knowledge at lower levels of aggregation and the increased degree of accuracy that pharmacogenomic technologies may provide could strain the means by which decisions about pharmaceutical coverage are currently made.

That more precise and accurate knowledge poses a challenge to an existing regulatory setting is somewhat contrary to the findings of Lakoff. His study of efforts to identify genetic markers for bipolar disease in Argentina makes visible the close intertwining of fundamental notions of disease causality with the regulation and production of knowledge about psychiatric treatment regimens and the organization and undertaking of clinical care. Notably, he highlights the pervasive influence of 'pharmaceutical reason' (Lakoff 2006, 6–7) on a wide range of actors. This strategic logic operates with the underlying rationale of linking drugs directly to diagnosis. Citing Rosenberg (2002), Lakoff characterizes this rationale as 'disease specificity' (2006, 158–9), according to which illnesses are understood as stable entities which can be explained through universal causal mechanisms that are identifiable in the bodies of sufferers. Of particular relevance is my understanding of disease specificity as a tool of administrative management that makes it possible to rationalize health practices through the production of standardized evidence of treatment efficacy (a development discussed by Berg 1997; Pope 2003; Timmermans and Berg 2003). Lakoff concludes that pharmacogenomic technologies support the norm of specificity as evoked in regulatory arrangements since 'genomic technology seeks to make the [specificity] model more accurate. Pharmacogenomics serve as a mechanism of adjustment between drug and disease entity – a way of calibrating intervention more closely to illness' (Lakoff 2006, 174). This characterization of pharmacogenomics suggests that the momentum of pharmaceuticalization could be further enhanced by a more widespread availability of individualized drug-based treatments. While Lakoff goes on to illustrate how more precise calibrations of drugs to diseases may clash with other configurations of functionality – notably those found in clinical practices; see also Hedgecoe (2008) on the usefulness of pharmacogenomic technologies as a situated achievement – I argue that disease specificity is also a difficult norm to adhere to in a regulatory setting. A widespread commercial availability of individualized pharmaceutical treatments is therefore likely to have more diverse implications for the manner in which pharmaceuticals are situated and the momentum of pharmaceuticalization.

The following empirical account will inquire into how the Swedish Dental and Pharmaceutical Benefits Agency (henceforth 'TLV', the same agency discussed in the previous chapter) makes decisions about conventional drugs. The organization's classification of pharmaceuticals as included or excluded from the public pharmaceutical benefits scheme mobilizes particular modes of characterizing and categorizing patients, diseases and drug-based therapies. Foregrounding the means by which the TLV characterizes and categorizes 'treatable' patients and 'reimbursable' pharmaceutical use contributes to the final purpose of this chapter: to articulate the versions of solidarity that are produced. Previous studies illustrate how the regulatory setting can have a considerable influence on how legitimate uses and abuses of biotechnology are defined and materialized (see, for example, Jasanoff 2005; Prainsack and Firestine 2006). As previously mentioned, the delineation of coverage is a practical concern in both publicly and privately funded local health care systems. This is because a balance between individual and aggregate needs for treatment is a fundamental problem for any attempt to undertake a just distribution of limited resources – irrespective of how this justice is defined. Nevertheless, this matter arguably has particular salience in welfare systems with espoused ideals of 'universal coverage'. Here the boundary for collective fiscal responsibility[2] for individuals' health care needs must be drawn in a manner that is perceived as just and equitable. This is part of the construction and maintenance of a systemic solidarity, on which any such health care system depends. It is therefore important to understand the mechanisms whereby patients, diseases and pharmaceuticals are categorized in the process of determining coverage, as the scope of the public pharmaceutical benefits scheme has direct consequences for what manner of solidarity is achieved.

In the forthcoming empirical account, I follow how the TLV evaluates the reimbursement status of various non-pharmacogenomic pharmaceuticals. The decision to study conventional pharmaceuticals is partly premised on the limited experience of evaluating pharmacogenomic technologies' coverage. However, the evaluation uncertainties related to pharmacogenomic technologies are similar to other innovations (Ling and Raven 2006). Furthermore, previous sociologically informed studies of pharmacogenomics in practice lend support to the supposition that such technologies become 'ordinary' when embedded in existing organizational arrangements (Hedgecoe 2004, 7). Thus, the difficulties faced when evaluating conventional pharmaceuticals can be used to indicate potential challenges to ambitions of a more widespread introduction of pharmacogenomic drugs.

The remainder of this chapter is organized as follows. The next section will introduce the empirical setting of the study and then account for four controversies centred on the evaluation of pharmaceutical-based treatments for stomach acid–related disorders, migraines and erectile dysfunction. In each case, the focus is on incoherence between the level of aggregation and the degree of accuracy with which patients, diseases and pharmaceuticals are characterized, categorized and linked. The following section will discuss how these incoherencies are addressed and what forms of solidarity this produces.

Different categories or not? Dealing with incoherent characterizations of patients and pharmaceutical use

The Dental and Pharmaceutical Benefits Board: an organization to set boundaries for publicly funded pharmaceutical spending in Sweden

Whether patients must pay for their prescription pharmaceutical use can have potentially far-reaching effects on usage patterns. This is perhaps most obviously the case in welfare states, where patients' out-of-pocket expenditure for drugs has historically been low and the reimbursement of pharmaceutical use relates to an overarching concern with fair and equitable resource allocation. How to prioritize resources is an enduring concern in the field of health care. In recent decades, the debate over resource allocation within health care has tended to take its point of departure in the perception of a widening gap between the supply and demand of health care intervention. This has brought the question of prioritization to the fore, whether between different forms of medical interventions or between different therapy areas and patient groups.

One way many Western welfare states have sought to address the question of which treatments to provide and reimburse is through the creation of central health care technology assessment (HTA) organizations. These organizations typically have instructions which emphasize the use of scientific facts in decision-making (Jost 2005). The organized collection and evaluation of evidence about treatment effects is conceived as a means to achieve a more fair and effective prioritization of limited resources (Cuyler and Newhouse 2000; Mitton and Donaldson 2004). The creation of HTA organizations as such is therefore in line with the pervasive idea that the evidence-based standardization of treatment decisions and medical clinical practice can secure broadly defined better outcomes (Drori *et al.* 2003; Pope 2003; Timmermans and Berg 2003).

In Sweden, a governmental agency was created in 2002 with the task of determining the reimbursement status of all prescription pharmaceuticals.[3] Prior to the creation of the TLV, all use of prescription pharmaceuticals in Sweden was 'automatically subsidized' (New Pharmaceutical Benefits Bill 2001, 1).[4] According to the TLV's governing legislation, pharmaceuticals should now be granted reimbursement when:

> the cost for using the pharmaceutical . . . is reasonable from medical, humanitarian and socio-economic perspectives.
> (Act on Pharmaceutical Benefits, Section 15)

When a pharmaceutical is excluded from the pharmaceutical benefits scheme, patients must pay for all outpatient use of the product.[5] In contrast, the cost of a pharmaceutical that has been approved for reimbursement is carried by the patients' counties of residence.[6] The legislation gives the TLV the option to approve reimbursement for restricted uses of a drug. However, this alternative is to be used sparingly in order to uphold the principle of a product-based reimbursement system (Act on Pharmaceutical Benefits, Section 11).

The work of the TLV to decide pharmaceuticals' reimbursement status is divided between the Board and the Bureau. The Board has the formal decision-making power. The government appoints its eleven members to reflect different interest groups within the health care sector (Ordinance with Instructions for the Pharmaceutical Benefits Board, Section 8). Present and previous Board members include practising general physicians, health economists, medical specialists, medical ethicists, individuals with experience from patient organizations and county health administrators. The role of the Bureau is to undertake evaluations to support the Board in its decision-making. The Bureau employs approximately fifty individuals, many of whom hold doctorates in pharmacy or health economics.

By law, the TLV must publicly justify its decision outcomes in so-called decision justification documents. However, as it is not specified what it means for a pharmaceutical to have a reasonable cost of use, the onus is on the TLV to make decisions that can be publicly justified as being in accordance with the agency's governing legislation. The legislative bill submitted to Parliament provides some guidance for interpreting the legal framework. As mentioned in the previous chapter, the bill instructs the TLV to adopt 'a broad approach' (Pharmaceutical

Benefits Bill 2001, 46) and to take into consideration the three principles of priority setting that Parliament approved in 1997. These are: *equal human value*, meaning all people have an equal right to life and health; *need solidarity*, that those with greatest need of treatment have priority over those with lesser need; and *cost-effectiveness*, that the benefit of treatment must be reasonable in relation to its cost (Socialutskottet 1997). There are no detailed instructions about what it means in practice to take these principles into consideration. However, the agency is explicitly encouraged to use health economic techniques for evaluating drugs (New Pharmaceutical Benefits Bill 2001). Notably, the TLV must not take into consideration the budgetary impact of implementing its decisions. Nor does the agency have any targets to fulfil as regards the level of pharmaceutical spending.

The following section describes four instances of conflicting characterizations and categorizations of treatable patients and reimbursable pharmaceutical use. Three of these accounts are based on a detailed study of the evaluation of pharmaceuticals for the treatment of migraine and two stomach acid–related disorders. These decision-making processes were followed using a combination of fifty-seven semi-structured interviews with members of the TLV's two project groups and members of the organization's decision-making Board, analysis of working documents and decision justification documents and participant observation (described in greater detail in Sjögren 2006, 59–67). Following the completion of this study, the resulting controversy concerning one decision outcome was opportunistically identified and followed via articles selected through key word searches in a proprietary media database (Mediearkivet). The fourth account looks at the legal appeal of the TLV's denial of reimbursement for Viagra. The empirical material derives from the TLV's decision justification documents and the various court rulings in the case (for a more detailed discussion of methodology, see Chapter 2).

In each account, the focus is on how the TLV deals with incoherencies which emerge between different levels of aggregation and degrees of accuracy when characterizing and categorizing patients, diseases and drug use. The first account is from the stomach-acid group, where the TLV had to address the significant prescription of certain pharmaceuticals to 'untreatable' patients.

Identifying 'untreatable' patients: sorting similar symptoms into different diagnosis categories?

The stomach-acid group was one of two pilot projects for the TLV's review of the existing pharmaceutical assortment. It was launched in October 2003. At an early stage, members of the stomach-acid group described a 'well-known' problem of off-label prescription. The specific suspicion was that physicians were prescribing a class of drugs called proton pump inhibitors (PPIs) to patients who had *stomach-ache* rather than *gastro-oesophageal reflux disease* (GERD). These two conditions could have similar symptoms. However, numerous sources agreed that only patients with GERD could be successfully treated with PPIs. Unfortunately, it was often difficult for clinicians to determine whether a patient had GERD:

> Everything else is clear-cut . . . you have a bacterial infection; you have an ulcerous sore, and so on. With GERD, there is so much variation. . . . You have symptoms with sores, sores but no symptoms, symptoms with no sores.[7]

It was considered problematic that the means of identifying 'treatable' patients was so ambiguous.[8] In an attempt to resolve this ambiguity, the stomach-acid group proposed that the Board restrict reimbursement of PPIs to patients with a confirmed diagnosis of GERD. In order to ensure a confirmed diagnosis, the suggestion was to make reimbursement of treatment for patients with GERD contingent on a gastroscopic examination. However, the Board ultimately discarded this and other suggestions to delimit a smaller category of treatable patients linked to reimbursed drug use. Instead, all of the PPIs were included in the pharmaceutical benefits scheme. Informants explained that this outcome was largely a consequence of the Board's recognition that it was not possible for the TLV to intervene in diagnostic practices in the manner needed to make a more specific category of 'reimbursed pharmaceutical use' stable and feasible to implement in clinical practice:

> The Board took a pragmatic view and said that we can't tell the doctors how they should make a diagnosis . . . we don't know enough about what it would mean, what kind of equipment they have access to today.[9]

Had the Board chosen to include a restriction in line with the Bureau's original proposal, this could have become a 'hard strike in the air'.[10] This would have been potentially problematic for the perceived legitimacy of the TLV's work.

Furthermore, informants noted that if the Board were to take differences in diagnosis-related treatment regimens into consideration for the case of PPIs there was a strong likelihood that more reimbursement decisions would have specific inclusion criteria. The widespread use of diagnosis-based reimbursement restrictions was not in line with the principle of a product-based system for pharmaceutical reimbursement, which the TLV's governing legislation instructed the organization to uphold (New Pharmaceutical Benefits Bill 2001, 37–8). One informant noted that it was a principal problem that a product-based system inferred that all pharmaceuticals had only *one* cost and effect, which could be clearly measured and systematically evaluated.[11] That a pharmaceutical in practice might have *multiple* effects (and costs) related to the treatment of *different* patient groups was not in line with the legislation's basic premise.

In summary, the TLV discarded the possibility of formulating more specific inclusion criteria for patients with GERD in the face of epistemological problems with delineating a correct, stable and clinically feasible category of patients with this diagnosis. Formulating a more specific inclusion criterion was also at odds with the principle of a product-based reimbursement system. By approving reimbursement for all the PPIs, the TLV constructed a broadly inclusive category of treatable patients. The ambiguity concerning who belonged to this category and should have their pharmaceutical use reimbursed was delegated to medical practitioners. A similar strategy of delegating ambiguity was used to resolve incoherency in the comparison of treatment effects for products in the migraine group.

From one comparison to none: the failure to match the treatment effect of migraine drugs to stable patient groups

In the preceding account, the identification of specific 'treatable' patients was delegated to medical practitioners. The challenge in the migraine group was somewhat different, since there were no perceived problems for clinicians to diagnose patients with migraine. Therefore, the TLV's migraine group initially intended to evaluate the treatment effects of different pharmaceuticals using data from various clinical trials. However, it soon became apparent that this data was incoherent. Notably, the studies used different measurements of treatment effect and also defined different categories of 'comparable' drugs. This made it impossible to make a general comparison of all the drugs using a common metric. To resolve this problem, the Bureau's project group decided to use the golden standard for measuring treatment effect as defined by the International Headache Society. As most clinical trials included this metric, it could be used to compare some – if not all – results from the studies.[12]

Once the comparable effect metric had been defined, the subsequent evaluation was initially couched as a matter of deciding how many pharmaceuticals were needed to ensure adequate product diversity. One project member likened this to an analysis of 'marginal rate of return', where the first product might treat a certain percentage of patients and subsequent pharmaceuticals could treat an increasingly smaller group of new patients.[13] However, the project group's seconded medical experts and various other parties soon highlighted a critical problem: it was not possible to foresee which patient would respond to which pharmaceutical within a chemically similar group of drugs called triptanes. This meant that '[i]n practice, doctor and patient must test until a triptane with good effect and acceptable tolerance is identified' (TLV 2005a, 23). Since the triptanes were not interchangeable treatment alternatives for identifiable groups of patients, it was not possible to compare their treatment effect using the chosen metric.[14] The failure to compare treatment effects, in combination with the high-calculated cost of not treating migraine, was described by informants as a strong contributing factor behind the TLV's subsequent approval of reimbursement for all the triptanes. Yet, while the TLV approved reimbursement for all of these drugs, the agency's final report for the migraine group also included a ranking of the evaluated pharmaceuticals in order of calculated cost-effectiveness. It was stressed that the ranking was not a general treatment recommendation and the TLV would not monitor compliance to the ranking, However, the intention was that the ranking could guide medical practitioners in choosing an order in which to test the triptanes.

> If one took cost-effectiveness into consideration. But there are other things that need to be taken into account as well, of course.
>
> (Interview project manager migraine group, 22 February 2005)

The preceding example from the stomach-acid group revealed problems with defining a stable category of 'treatable' patients using a diagnosis-specific inclusion criterion. In the present case, the migraine group struggled with how to establish a stable and coherent characterization of the evaluated pharmaceuticals. An intended comparison of treatment effects was thwarted due to a failure to achieve comparable data. This failure resulted from the lack of a stable object of knowledge: there was no aggregate of patients for whom the treatment effects of different drugs could be compared. Instead of identifiable patient groups, there were individual patients with different and unforeseeable responses to treatment. The TLV's solution to this ambiguity was to forego any specific inclusion criteria that might risk the exclusion of pharmaceuticals that were potentially the only treatment alternative for certain patients. Instead, a broad category of reimbursable drug use was established. The work to characterize and categorize a particular tripane as appropriate to reimburse when used by a specific patient was delegated to medical practitioners.

In summary, both of the preceding cases saw the delegation of ambiguity over the characterization and categorization of treatable patients and reimbursable drug use to medical practitioners. In the following example, concerns over the feasibility of implementing reimbursement restrictions in clinical practice meant that such delegation was not considered appropriate.

'A few good men' are not enough: the exclusion of Viagra from the pharmaceutical benefits scheme

As detailed in the previous chapter, in March 2008, the Supreme Administrative Court of Sweden ruled to exclude Viagra (and two other pharmaceuticals used for the treatment of erectile dysfunction) from the public pharmaceutical benefits scheme. This decision ended a process that had started seven years earlier, when the Swedish government decided to immediately cease general reimbursement of Viagra. In the aftermath of a heated public debate, the government took steps to reverse its decision. Less than six months later, the TLV began its operations. The reimbursement status of Viagra was one of the first cases the new agency decided. In March 2003, Viagra was once again excluded from coverage. The decision justification document issued by the agency gave two reasons for this outcome.

The first argument was that Viagra was not generally reasonable to reimburse for treatment of all forms of erectile dysfunction. Notably, the TLV argued that the medical studies cited in the application for reimbursement showed neither that the product was *generally cost-effective* nor for *which particular patient groups* the drug was cost-effective (TLV 2003, 4). The second argument was that no dependable way exists to identify specific groups of treatable patients that could be deemed societally reasonable to provide with reimbursed treatment. Had this been possible, the TLV might have approved reimbursement for Viagra to patients with severe erectile dysfunction. However, the perceived inability of medical practitioners to determine the medically treatable *and* societally reasonable patients made it necessary to deny reimbursement to all patients.

As described in Chapter 2, the company marketing Viagra appealed the TLV's decision and a series of court battles ensued. Prior to the Supreme Court's ruling, two lower courts overturned the TLV's decision and approved restricted reimbursement for Viagra for a specific category of patients. The Lower Court defined this category as patients with certain medical conditions such as diabetes or cardiovascular diseases, or patients who were prescribed the drug by a urologist (Stockholm County Administrative Court 2004). While the TLV's subsequent appeal of the Lower Court's ruling was not upheld, the Appellant Court *did* change the category of patients to be included in coverage. Instead of a primarily diagnosis-based categorization, the Appellant Court restricted reimbursement to initial prescription by a medical specialist on male reproductive organs. The court described this as a more dependable way of identifying the medically treatable and societally reasonable patients (Stockholm Administrative Court of Appeals 2005).

Three years later, the Supreme Administrative Court justified its denial of all reimbursement on three grounds (Supreme Administrative Court of Sweden 2008):

1 The existence of two alternative treatments for patients with severe erectile dysfunction [i.e. those patients who were both treatable and reasonable to provide with reimbursed treatment; author's note]
2 The uncertainty of a diagnosis for severe erectile dysfunction, and
3 The imagined behaviours of patients and doctors that created a clear risk for off-label prescription of Viagra to patients other than those whom it was 'reasonable' to treat with reimbursed pharmaceuticals.

The Supreme Court's second and third arguments are similar to those the TLV made in its original decision justification document. The perceived risk, that medical practitioners would be too inclusive when categorizing patients as eligible for reimbursed Viagra, justified the exclusion of all Viagra use from coverage.

In summary, the first two cases centred on various problems that the TLV had with creating correct and stable categories of treatable patients and reimbursable drug use that were feasible to implement in clinical practice. In both the migraine and stomach-acid groups, the epistemological problem of characterizing, categorizing and matching patients, diseases and drugs was delegated to medical practitioners through the delineation of broad, inclusive categories. As argued in Chapter 2, the case of Viagra further illustrates how the basis for characterization and categorization needed to be stable and feasible to implement in clinical practice. The fourth and final example elaborates further on the issue of clinical feasibility by looking at the implementation of a TLV decision for a specific patient group.

Ensuring reimbursed pharmaceutical use for a deserving few: implementing the decision to exclude all Losec use from coverage

Since its inception, the TLV has evaluated hundreds of products. While most decisions have met with few public reactions, this account concerns one case which did become a matter of some public attention: the general exclusion of Losec from coverage. Losec, a brand-name pharmaceutical in the stomach-acid group, was deemed unreasonable to subsidize on the grounds that other products with the same active substance had a significantly lower price. These drugs were interchangeable with Losec, according to the list maintained by the Swedish Medical Products Agency. Thus, the TLV argued that patients could receive another product when filling their Losec prescriptions. The result would be significant cost savings, without a loss of treatment quality.

However, in the aftermath of the TLV's decision in February 2006, reports surfaced about an unforeseen consequence of excluding Losec from coverage. The TLV's decision was based on the fact that patients using Losec could remain in treatment with another brand of drug. This premise was derived in part from an analysis of data from clinical trials and sales statistics, which suggested that a number of products were interchangeable for the patient population using Losec. However, information now surfaced about a group of patients for which Losec was the only treatment option. This patient group was young children with GERD. They had difficulties swallowing capsules and therefore needed to take the active ingredient in a form that could be broken apart and softened.

The exclusion of this group of patients from reimbursed treatment was not considered a reasonable outcome. Several counties' solution was to finance this particular use of Losec through an alternative route. Specifically, the Losec these patients used was re-categorized as *inpatient* use. By doing so, the counties managed to put in place a number of extra routines so that the National Corporation of Pharmacies could directly bill the cost to the counties.

In summary, this final case makes visible the incoherence between different levels of aggregation and degrees of accuracy in both the characterization and categorization of patients, and the matching of patient categories with pharmaceuticals. The data the TLV used crafted a large category of patients for whom the active substance – not a particular brand or dosage form – was important for treatability. But this category was not stable in other settings. Specifically, it clashed with a more fine-grained category of patients in medical practice for whom dosage form was a key component of treatability. To ensure that the treatment of these patients remained reimbursed, a new organizational arrangement was put in place. This involved the re-categorization of Losec from outpatient to inpatient use. Thus, the inclusion of the specific category of patients in coverage was achieved outside the regulatory arrangements of the pharmaceutical benefits scheme.

The following section will compare and contrast the four accounts of how incoherent and unstable categorizations of treatable patients and reimbursable drugs were addressed. The focus is on the mechanisms for resolving ambiguities, and on the consequences for inclusion and exclusion that these solutions provide.

Discussion

The four preceding accounts illustrate various detailed and case-specific problems related to the evaluation of reimbursement status for pharmaceutical-based treatments of stomach acid–related disorders, migraine and erectile dysfunction. However, the examples also highlight common challenges in the TLV's work to appropriately and reliably create and maintain stable categories of 'treatable' patients, and link these patients with 'societally reasonable' pharmaceutical use in line with the legal criteria for reimbursement. I will now discuss how perceived epistemological problems in this categorization work were addressed. The second part of the section will elaborate on the difficulty of achieving high disease specificity when making decisions about coverage. The final part of the section will relate the observed processes of decision-making about pharmaceutical reimbursement to the production of different modes of solidarity.

Making decisions with ambiguous knowledge by delegating ambiguity to others

In the first case, the TLV struggled with how to differentiate between 'treatable' and 'untreatable' patients in its reimbursement decisions for drugs in the stomach-acid group. The Bureau project group made various proposals to delimit a more specific category of patients with the 'treatable' disease GERD. One example was the suggestion to make reimbursement contingent on a 'confirmed diagnosis'. This was defined as a diagnosis made after a gastroscopic exam. However, the Board discarded these suggestions. In part, this behaviour can be attributed to the Board's recognition of a lack of supporting technologies. Notably, the Board was aware that lack of access to gastroscopes could impede the implementation of such a restriction. In foregoing more specific inclusion criteria in its decision outcome, the TLV delegated ambiguity over which specific individuals were to be categorized as treatable patients to medical practitioners.

The second account of the migraine group described work to characterize and categorize pharmaceuticals using a comparison of treatment effect. By deciding to use the International Headache Society's metric, the TLV defined an ostensibly common means of measuring treatment effect. This opened up the possibility of formulating more narrowly defined criteria for what could be categorized as 'reimbursable' drug use. Yet this means for comparing drugs broke down in later stages of the decision-making process, when the TLV was unable to sustainably link the measurements of treatment effect to a stable and identifiable patient population. The subsequent decision to approve reimbursement for all the trip-tanes can also be described as delegation to medical practitioners: this time of the work to determine whether a given pharmaceutical made a patient treatable, and thus made the drug reasonable to prescribe with reimbursement.

The first two cases illustrate how attempts to craft more specific categories of treatable patients and reasonable drugs were abandoned in favour of broadly inclusive decision outcomes that delegated the ambiguity of categorization to medical practitioners. The story of Viagra reads differently. Despite a widespread agreement about the existence of a specific group of patients that merited reimbursed use of Viagra (individuals with severe erectile dysfunction), this characterization of patients was not deemed stable and feasible in clinical practice. The agency doubted the ability of medical practitioners to appropriately limit the prescription of Viagra to these deserving few. Rather than the broadly inclusive category in the previous two cases, the outcome in the Viagra case was a broadly *exclusive* category that made it necessary for all patients to take private fiscal responsibility for their Viagra use.

While this chapter does not consider what responses the denial of Viagra may have triggered, the final case of Losec offers insight into how an ostensibly stable category of treatable patients was upset *after* the TLV had made its reimbursement decision. The agency's decision to exclude Losec from the pharmaceutical benefits scheme was premised on the comparison of treatment effects within a patient population for whom the active substance defined treatability. The subsequent breakdown of this category of patients – which had been sourced from clinical trials – came in the intersection with a particular clinical practice. Suddenly there was a specific group of patients whose treatability was closely entwined with Losec as a specific product. This group of patients had not been rendered visible for the TLV. Following the TLV's decision, efforts were made by other parties to *de facto* include the specific patient group in coverage.

The four accounts provide examples of how the TLV dealt with ambiguity to reach a decision outcome. To make a decision that could be justified, there was a need for the characterization and categorization of patients, diseases and drugs to be correct, stable and feasible to implement in clinical practice. If this was difficult to achieve, then an alternative recourse was for the TLV to remove ambiguity about who was a treatable patient and what was reimbursable drug use through delegation to others, notably medical practitioners (see also Rappert 2001). In the first case from the stomach-acid group, members of the TLV's Bureau and Board expressed a practical understanding of the socio-technical network of clinical work. Thus, the requirement to have a confirmed diagnosis in order to reimburse pharmaceutical treatment of GERD was discarded since it was dependant on a supporting network of elements, such as a gastroscope, which the agency could not mobilize. The justification that certain Viagra use could not be granted restricted reimbursement due to concerns over compliance similarly reflects an understanding of diagnosis as a situated accomplishment, which can be malleable to the influence of different actors. These examples thus illustrate how more precise and detailed knowledge about patient subgroups and their treatment responses did not immediately and automatically resolve the challenge of justifying decisions based on correct, stable and clinically feasible knowledge.

'Specific' concerns in crafting categories of included and excluded patients and pharmaceuticals

The preceding section discussed the TLV's responses to ambiguity in the characterization and categorization of patients, diseases and pharmaceuticals. Arguably, one foundation for the aforementioned epistemological problems is the codified norm of disease specificity (Rosenberg 2002, cited in Lakoff 2006). This is most clearly made visible in the description of the legally sanctioned product-based reimbursement system as a model which assumes each drug has one set of treatment effects which can be attributed to a clearly defined patient population. This assumption is recurrently challenged in the preceding four accounts. Nevertheless, the option of formulating more specific inclusion criteria for coverage appears to be a comparatively weak one. This might be the case for several reasons.

One obvious reason is that the legislation governing the agency's work instructs it to strive to uphold a product-based reimbursement system. However, a further explanation is that the agency lacks the means of influencing the work practices of medical practitioners. The TLV has no mechanisms to ensure compliance to any more specific restrictions it might set out. A third reason, highlighted by the problem of diagnosing GERD and prescribing migraine drugs with treatment effect, is that adhering to the underlying assumption of disease specificity when making decisions about coverage makes it problematic for the TLV to both justify decisions based on evidence, as is required by law, *and* reach outcomes that can be appropriately implemented in clinical practice, in line with its intended task of setting priorities for public pharmaceutical spending. This dual imperative makes it difficult to disregard knowledge from either clinical trials or clinical practice. This creates a basis for clashes between the level of aggregation and degree of accuracy with which patients and pharmaceuticals are possible to characterize and categorize. It is against this backdrop that the advent of pharmacogenomic technologies should be considered.

What this chapter suggests is that a greater accuracy at lower levels of aggregation than pharmacogenomic technologies could provide would further strain the construction of stable objects of regulatory intervention. The difficulties of rendering stable representations of patients that can encompass variation – notably as regards diagnosis practices and treatment response – contributes to blurring the category of medically treatable, societally reasonable and therefore *regulate-able* patients. Thus, in contrast to earlier conclusions about the capacity for pharmacogenomic technologies to support a further calibration of health care rationalization (Lakoff 2006, 174) and provide momentum to pharmaceuticalization, the present study suggests a potentially more destabilizing effect. Disease specificity is a difficult norm to adhere to in the current regulatory practice. A more precise knowledge about how to characterize and categorize treatable patients and reasonable drugs is not obviously more useable and useful when reaching a decision outcome. Rather, one could argue that the possibility of articulating a greater form of disease specificity *in certain forms of knowledge* could further contribute to the need for delegation of ambiguity and the attendant distribution of responsibility that this entails. However, the viability of this practice can be questioned. First, the possibility for *ad hoc* tinkering in those situations where unreasonable outcomes result from decisions about coverage, as exemplified by the case of Losec, does not provide – much less guarantee – a systematic treatment of such problems. Second, an increased ambition to standardize, control and direct the content of medical practice using evidence-based policy would make tinkering difficult to maintain (Berg 1997; Berg and Mol 1998; Timmermans and Berg 2003). The present inquiry into the construction and workings of a particular 'redistributive machinery' thus provides a basis for reflecting on both the existing production of solidarity, and what the advent of more individualized treatment and diagnosis could portend.

Inclusive forms of evidence-based solidarity?

This chapter highlights a possible underlying 'dysfunctional norm of disease specificity' in decision-making concerning resource allocation in the Swedish health care system. These findings suggest that pharmaceuticals which allow for more individually targeted therapy could make it even more complicated and potentially controversial to make such a local 'redistributive machinery' work. However, it would appear to be a difference of degree, rather than kind. The four accounts discussed earlier concern the evaluation of reimbursement status for conventional drugs. By analogy, it could be argued that technological advances – in particular when paired with more knowledge claims about matters such as individual patients' drug responses – might exacerbate the prevalence of upsetting precision in the Swedish context. This argument is supported, in part, by the results of a comparative study of how Germany, the Netherlands and the United Kingdom have incorporated three kinds of genetic technologies (Aarden 2009).

Based on a comparison of the local regulatory and medical practices by which medical technologies become available to individuals, Germany has a reticent pattern of provision for such technologies due to the relative importance of policy decision-making about health care provision. In these processes, cost-effectiveness and efficacy play an important role, such that the requirement for inclusion is tangible proof of disease or risk (Aarden 2009, 145). In a broader setting in which evidence-based decision-making is emphasized, this would tend to exclude groups of patients or pharmaceuticals for which evidence is unavailable or incoherent or where diagnosis and treatment in clinical practice remains complex and variable. This contrasts with the case of the Netherlands and the United Kingdom, where other forms of solidarity are achieved through practices that lead to the emphasis of alternative levels of specificity, for example of niche communities that match patients and technologies in the case of the Netherlands (ibid., 146).

The current study in Sweden suggests a tendency to forego the incorporation of more specific knowledge and inclusion criteria into decision outcomes in favour of broadly inclusive or exclusive categorizations of patients and pharmaceutical use. This could be taken to suggest that the solidarity such arrangements produce remains true to a principle of universal coverage. However, such a judgement must also take into consideration the settings into which decisions are implemented. As previously mentioned, at the time of the study the TLV had no responsibility for considering the financial impact of its decisions. A changed requirement that evaluations of public coverage should consider not only cost-effectiveness but also *economic* feasibility would arguably also limit the possibility of making broadly inclusive decisions at the policy level (see also discussion in Rai 2002). Similarly, the linking of remuneration to health care service providers to compliance with treatment guidelines and reimbursement decisions would arguably contribute to limiting the room for interpretation when implementing decisions in clinical practice. Such developments could become topical in a setting where the widespread expectation and fear is that conventional and pharmacogenomic technologies will continue to drive the direct cost of pharmaceutical-based treatment.

Conclusions

This chapter has inquired into a national governmental agency's efforts to include or exclude prescription drugs from a national pharmaceutical benefits scheme. I draw attention to the challenge ambiguous knowledge poses in the work of crafting stable categories of treatable patients and reimbursable drug use with which to justify local coverage decisions. The effort on the part of the studied agency to craft correct, stable and clinically feasible categories within a regulatory framework premised on disease specificity resulted in decisions with broadly inclusive or exclusive categories. The former type of decisions involves a delegation of ambiguity regarding the characterization and categorization of treatable patients and reimbursable drug use to medical practitioners. I have argued that different levels of aggregation and degrees of accuracy in knowledge claims about patients, diseases and pharmaceuticals are a potential source of 'upset' in categorization work. The observed delegation of ambiguity balances the dual need to make and justify evidence-based decisions which are feasible to implement in clinical practice. However, such outcomes are not obviously in line with the legislative ambitions to centrally prioritize resource allocation.

This study illustrates how a governmental agency's efforts to include or exclude drugs from a national pharmaceuticals benefits scheme is normative work that takes part in a wider politics of distribution for health care resources. A critical issue is how the dynamic tensions which emerge in the work of constructing locally reasonable and legitimate coverage decisions are addressed. This arguably requires an understanding of the mutual constitution of medical technologies and the distributive practices embedded within any local health care system. In particular, it implies sensitivity to the broader range of mechanisms and arenas through which new technologies in health care practices are situated, beyond the clinical setting. A related concern is how to make visible the normative work of organizations such as the TLV. Little visible public debate concerning the TLV's work exists in

Sweden. This contrasts with the experience in many other countries, where the work of HTA organizations has prompted controversy. For example, several decisions by the British National Institute for Clinical Excellence (NICE) have been the target of public outcry and the visible involvement of various advocacy groups (Moreira 2010). The lack of conflicts and visible interest group involvement in the Swedish case is partly a methodological artefact of the study, which focuses on the internal workings of the TLV. However, it is also an empirical finding that has thematic antecedents linked to the localization of technologies. In a comparative study of regulatory responses to agricultural biotechnology and GM food in Germany, the United States and the United Kingdom, Jasanoff (2005) she observed differences in the topic and manner of controversy within each country. He explained the observed differences in part by differences of civic epistemology, the 'culturally specific, historically and politically grounded, public knowledge-ways' that encompass shared understandings of how knowledge should be 'presented, tested, verified, and put to use in public arenas' (Jasanoff 2005, 249, 256). In a similar vein, Prainsack and Firestine (2006) have argued that the absence of public controversies concerning biobanks in Israel is due to a series of narratives that construct biotechnology as crucial for the continuity of Jewish existence in the region.

The lack of visible conflict about TLV decisions in Sweden can also be attributed to the workings of a 'machinery' of social technologies and devices, which renders the TLV's decision-making processes opaque (Casula and Sjögren 2011) and formats the participation of interest groups (Sjögren and Fernler 2010). A publicly funded health care system is ultimately dependant on the boundaries for public fiscal responsibility being set in a manner that is perceived as legitimate. The present chapter highlights the complex interplay between scientific and clinical knowledge claims with different levels of aggregation and with varying degrees of accuracy, which gives rise to recurrent ambiguity as to how patients and interventions should be characterized, categorized and linked. This ambiguity must be addressed in order to construct stable categories of patients, diseases and drugs that can serve as objects for regulatory intervention. Building on previous chapters, the examples of Viagra and other conventional drugs highlight that the future of pharmaceutical access is not limited to enrolling participants in clinical practice but enrolling society to subsidize access to situated understandings of 'legitimate' drug use. Thus, even with a more incremental introduction of individualized technologies for diagnosis and treatment, there is an ongoing need to follow the avenues whereby they become embedded in existing local systems for deciding the scope and content of health care provision.

Notes

1 Substantive parts of this chapter have been previously published as Sjögren, Ebba (2010). Upsetting Categories? The Consequences of Pharmacogenomics for Making Knowledge-based Decisions in Sweden. *New Genetics and Society*, *29* (4), 389–411.

2 Public funding of health care can be supplied in various ways. One such method, which is in place in Sweden, is the direct provision or third party financing of health care services using taxes. An alternative model, which is used in Germany and Holland, is

based around statutory health insurance schemes (see Wagstaff *et al.* 1999 for a brief overview).

3 The term *pharmaceutical reimbursement* is commonly used in the literature. However, the term *subsidization status* more accurately captures the structure of the Swedish pharmaceutical benefits scheme. This scheme is designed to minimize private expenses in connection with illness. In the current set-up, a patient pays the full cost of prescription pharmaceuticals up to 1,100 SEK (approximately 112 Euro). A graduated subsidy then reduces the patient's direct cost for prescription medication so that (s)he never pays more than 2,200 SEK (approximately 225 Euro) in a twelve-month period.

4 The term was used to describe how a drug was included in the public pharmaceutical benefits scheme once the Swedish Medical Products Agency (or its European equivalent, EMEA) had approved it for use.

5 'Outpatient use' refers to pharmaceutical use, which takes place outside of monitored hospital care. This can include pharmaceuticals which have been prescribed during inpatient care, but which are intended for use after discharge from hospital. When a pharmaceutical is excluded from the pharmaceutical benefits scheme, this in no way limits the right of physicians to prescribe the drug. The use of pharmaceuticals for inpatient treatment is not subject to centralized regulation by the TLV. This coverage is decided by the individual counties.

6 The twenty-one counties finance the majority of health care services directly through an income tax levied on all county residents who are in paid employment. The cost of the pharmaceutical reimbursement is billed to patients' resident counties by the state-owned National Corporation of Swedish Pharmacies, which held a legally sanctioned monopoly on the distribution of pharmaceuticals in Sweden until 1 July 2009.

7 Interview project manager stomach-acid group, 17 May 2005.

8 Interview project manager stomach-acid group, 2 September 2005; interview health economist, 16 November 2005.

9 Interview project manager stomach-acid group, 23 November 2005.

10 Interview project manager stomach-acid group, 23 November 2005.

11 Interview health economist stomach-acid group, 28 September 2004.

12 Interview project manager migraine group, 10 June 2004. See also discussion about the lack of 'ideal effect metric' (TLV 2006, 41–2).

13 Interview project manager migraine group, 19 April 2004.

14 Interview health economist migraine group, 22 February 2005.

Part 2

Changes in the medical discourse

4 The Swedish medical discourse

Impotence, erectile dysfunction and Viagra in *Läkartidningen*[1]

Ericka Johnson

Medicalizing the ageing male

The inability to achieve and maintain an erection has had many causes and many cures. Ancient Greeks attributed it to a diet of dry, cooling foods. During the European Middle Ages, impotency could be the result of a curse – dealt out by one's enemies, a witch or a slighted lover who tied knots in a string. Later, sexual excess, youthful indulgences and masturbation were blamed. During the nineteenth century both a wife's aversion to sex and her desire for it could cause impotence, as well as a glimpse of her 'unattractive' female genitals. The stress of modern, urban living was (and still is) made a culprit. Then, of course, comes the litany of Oedipal urges, domineering mothers, incestuous fixations and the Freudian analysts needed to cure these. In the mid twentieth century, especially in the United States, therapists looked to relationship issues for a cause and the point of treatment, while in a wider arena impotence was variously attributed to feminism, the sexual revolution and the contraceptive pill. And most recently, impotence has become a vascular issue (for a cultural history of impotence, see McLaren 2007).

Tracing the changing expectations of men's potency and vitality in Europe and North America shows how male sexuality has, with time, become more and more medicalized. This is true of sexuality in general. It has slowly gained recognition as a field in medicine: conferences are being held about various aspects of sexuality; medical journals on the subject are sprouting up; medical schools are offering courses in sexuality and some are even opening entire departments in the field; doctors are being encouraged to speak with their patients about sexual histories during routine medical exams; and pharmaceutical solutions to sexual 'problems' help define these problems as medical (Fishman and Mamo 2001, 181; Tiefer 2006, 274f). At the same time, non-medical experts are flourishing, offering sexual advice on the Internet, radio talk shows and TV, in magazines and newspapers (Tiefer 2006, 275). But while female reproductive health has traditionally been a focus of medical intervention (see Martin 1992; Oudshoorn 1994; Dugdale 2000), for men it has been virility, with strength and vitality instead of reproductive capacity, that has long attracted medical attention (Sengoopta 2006; McLaren 2007).

Sexuality is not the only area of life to be medicalized and later pharmaceuticalized with the development of pharmaceutical solutions to health 'problems'. The processes of medicalization and pharmaceuticalization depend on the social and technical networks within which people and diseases are placed. As Oudshoorn states, 'health problems can only be classified as illness and be medicalized if there exists a cultural climate and a medical infrastructure that actively transforms health complaints into diseases' (Oudshoorn 1997, 143). Thus, solutions to problems like depression, anxiety, obesity, hair loss and ageing can become medical solutions when both the medical community and general population recognize them as such. This process is not uncontroversial, however, and the pharmaceutical solutions to obesity, hair loss and ageing can be grouped together with the treatment for erectile dysfunction in the category of drugs sometimes called lifestyle drugs (Mamo and Fishman 2001, 16; Elliott 2003; Loe 2004a; Moynihan and Cassels 2005; Williams *et al.* 2011a). While some of these cures address problems that most people would at least nowadays call diseases (like depression), the disease status of others is more contested and their development has spawned the term *disease mongering* to denote the process of medicalization that uses medical practice and medical technologies to promote a concept of improvement unto perfection and the idea of medication for instant, scientific solutions for physiological and psychological distress (see Fishman 2004, 193; Tiefer 2006, 274). Disease mongering not only serves the purposes of pharmaceutical companies looking for conditions that can fit their pharmaceutical cures, it also expands the areas of life that doctors can claim as their territory – and for which they can charge consultation fees and sell drugs (Elliott 2003).

Some of these lifestyle drugs and diseases are related to a change in attitudes towards activity, sexual and otherwise, in older age. The concept of successful ageing allows the medical community to offer medical solutions to health problems traditionally associated with ageing, problems like hair loss, menopause and, as will be discussed in this chapter, erectile dysfunction. As the medical community claims these areas as its domain (rather than the domain of diet, witchcraft, antisocial behaviour or psychoanalysis, for example), the problems become diseases and the solutions are often decidedly medical, in the form of surgeries, drugs and physiological treatments. Because these solutions to ageing are creating diseases out of changes during the life span, the idea of getting older successfully has been critiqued for promoting an idea of ageing that really means not ageing at all (Marshall 2006, 350). Viagra and its promise of returning male sexual performance to a youthful, erection-on-demand state so that anyone can have sexual intercourse at any time and any age is currently one of the most talked about treatments for successful ageing.

This development should be placed in the history of medicalized male vitality. In the early part of the twentieth century, it was thought that the secret to masculine vitality was found in the sex glands, and much research about these glands, in both people and animals, was conducted (see Oudshoorn 1994; Marshall 2006; Sengoopta 2006). One of the medical treatments developed during the 1920s (sometimes called the decade of the testicle because of the intensity of research into testicles during this time) to treat a loss of vitality in ageing men was the Steinach operation. Developed by Austrian Eugen Steinach, and said to have been performed on both Freud and Yeats, the operation redirected fluid from the testicles to be reabsorbed into the body rather than released outside. This fluid was then thought to help revitalize the patients (Marshall 2006, 347; Sengoopta 2006; McLaren 2007). In the 1930s and 1940s, male rejuvenation treatments moved into more mainstream medical practices and began to reflect new knowledge about testosterone. Hormone therapy, that is testosterone treatment, was developed as a treatment for the 'male climacteric'. But again, the goal of treatment was general male vitality as displayed through physical and mental, but not necessarily sexual, prowess. In fact, increased sexual function was sometimes seen almost as an undesired and slightly embarrassing side effect of treatments (Marshall 2006, 347–8).

In the middle of the twentieth century, new research into sexuality and sexual behaviour changed the way sex and sexual dysfunction was perceived and treated. No longer was sexual decline in the male thought to be a natural part of ageing. Experts asserted that sexual activity and sexual intercourse were important parts of healthy ageing (Marshall 2006, 349). Impotence was thought to be caused by a fear of impotence. It was perceived as something that could be avoided and treated through therapy, often involving the partner, rather than through biomedical interventions (Tiefer 2006, 283). During the middle of the century and up into at least the 1980s, it was generally agreed that in 80% of impotence cases the problem was psychological and therapy was the best treatment.

According to feminist sex therapist Tiefer (2006), the psychology-based approach to sexuality in general and sexual dysfunction in particular changed during the 1980s. She notes that in the United States, several different factors contributed to a shift. For one thing, the American Psychiatric Association (APA) decided to define sexual problems as disorders in performing a sequence of genital functions, which coincided with a broader acceptance of a biomedical and psychopharmacological model of mental health. At the same time, the health industry began to use the *Diagnostic and Statistical Manual of Mental Disorders* and its definition of sexual (dys)function when determining which diseases would be eligible for reimbursement (Tiefer 2006, 283). Shortly thereafter, urology specialists began to take on more sexual dysfunction cases, which served to cement the idea that impotence was a biophysical issue of the penis, and led to examinations and treatments for sexual dysfunction that did not include the involvement of wives or partners (Tiefer 2006, 285).

Thus, impotence, which only a decade before had been called a psychological problem with physiological results, began to be seen as a physiological problem that could lead to psychological suffering (Marshall 2006, 350). The 1990s also saw other changes in the view of sexual dysfunction. Impotence became known as erectile dysfunction (ED), specifically located in the penis. By the late 1990s, largely thanks to research and advertising funded by Viagra's maker, Pfizer, the new reigning explanation for impotence stated that 70–80% of cases stemmed from physical causes, a direct reversal of the earlier ideas and one which supported medical consultations and prescription-based solutions rather than behavioural therapy or couples counselling (Plante 2006, 379). Sexual function was no longer seen as a controversial side effect of anti-ageing treatments; it was now the main goal.

The narrative of impotence and ED within the US context is also relevant to what has happened in Sweden, although with a bit of delay on some points. To examine the pharmaceuticalization of erectile dysfunction in this discourse in Sweden, I have analyzed articles dealing with impotence and erectile dysfunction in the generalist medical journal *Läkartidningen*.[2] I have looked at the articles published between 1990 and 2015, starting eight years before Viagra's introduction in 1998. Doing so shows that the construction of impotence, erectile dysfunction and male sexuality in *Läkartidningen* in some ways follows very closely with how these ideas have been framed in the international medical community, despite the framework of socialized medicine within which *Läkartidningen* publishes and the debates about subsidies of Viagra which have surrounded its introduction to the Swedish market. For example, in *Läkartidningen* the discourse has moved from social causes of impotence to a focus on mechanical and molecular aspects of ED, as has also happened in English-language journals. Reports in *Läkartidningen* from studies about impotence are also frequently linked to pharmaceutical funding after the introduction of Viagra, and there seems to be more column space granted to these discussions than there was before Viagra. In 2006, a study was published in *Läkartidningen* which reaffirmed that social aspects of ED contribute to individuals' treatment options. This suggests that a broader definition and re-evaluation of male sexuality could have appeared in the Swedish discourse. But it is rather unique. The local structures of health care provision also influenced the Viagra discourse in Sweden, framing it in debates about chronic medical conditions that produce 'legitimate' and severe ED. These debates are particularly Swedish in that they stem from questions about subsidizing Viagra with tax money.

Later I will present my analysis drawn from a careful reading of the *Läkartidningen* articles. In examining the articles, I have looked at the construction of patients and symptoms associated with impotence, as well as how the authors define and propose impotence and its cure(s). I have then contextualized this against results of similar analysis of the international discourse on impotence and ED. The articles studied have been found using the search words: impotence, impotence treatment, penis erection, erectile dysfunction, erectile difficulties, potency treatment, Viagra and Sildenafil.[3] A total of fifty-three articles was sourced for the years 1990–2015. Forty-five of these were published after Viagra was introduced.

Impotent patients before and after Viagra

Prior to Viagra, impotence was presented in *Läkartidningen* as a combination of psychological and physiological conditions. It was also something 'natural'. This understanding of the condition is reflected in a 1993 book review which asserts: 'Approximately ten percent of western men suffer from sexual difficulties associated with impotence, and if men can stay healthy and live long enough, they all become old-age-impotent'[4] (Mellgren 1993, 984). Old-age impotence, my translation for *åldersimpotent*, can be read as a specific type of impotence, and one that seems to disappear from the discourse after the arrival of Viagra and the presentation of the term *erectile dysfunction*. Also of note is that this number, 10%, is very low compared to Pfizer statistics that began to appear with the introduction of Viagra. (On the Viagra website,[5] ED is said to afflict more than half of men over fifty.)

Impotence, if natural, was, however, already a medicalized condition before Viagra arrived, although for fewer people. Pre-Viagra, impotence was also very complex in *Läkartidningen*. In an article about the causes of impotence from 1990, the authors spend an entire section speaking about feelings. They discuss the way men, particularly after not engaging in sex for a longer period of time, can want to have sex, but still not have sexual urges. They explain this by stating that 'many people interpret desire as the same thing as libido. But desire and libido are not the same thing' (Olsson *et al.* 1990, 4456). Five years later, in an article written by two of the same authors, the pre-Viagra discourse denied the feasibility and benefit of distinguishing between physical and emotional causes of impotence, something Viagra relies on. 'To create a distinction between somatic and psychological cases of impotence has been shown to match poorly with reality. Instead, one must for every patient evaluate biological factors and his feelings, his relationship to his partner, his family and work' (Olsson *et al.* 1995, 313). Thus, pre-Viagra, impotence is a result of a combination of (mostly social and emotional) factors.

It is not just the number of impotent patients and the emotional causes of impotence that change through the 1990s in *Läkartidningen*; the definition of an impotent patient also proves flexible. In the 1995 pre-Viagra article about impotence (Olsson *et al.*), impotent patients are constructed as a heterogeneous group, within which one finds some patients easier to treat than others. Those most likely to respond successfully to treatments are men in long-term relationships, and when discussing them, this 'patient' is frequently spoken about as the couple. More difficult to treat are single men, of which the authors identify three types: the young, shy man; the older man who has been sexually inactive for a while; and the loner carrying a secret. Of these, the older, sexually inactive man is seen as the easiest to treat (Olsson *et al.* 1995, 314). This typology of patients is based on social factors, and focuses on the men's relationships with others, not on the biological or mechanical causes of impotence. Respect for the social aspects of impotence also appears when, in the same article, the authors discuss reasons it can be difficult to treat impotent patients: because some impotent men can have rigid stereotypes about normal sexuality; they can find intimacy threatening; they think sex is about performance and thus develop performance anxiety; they are unable to recognize their own emotional signals; they see the ability to have intercourse as a sign of power; and/or because some of them experience impotence as shameful (Olsson *et al.* 1995, 314). And, as the authors later go on to say, the most difficult thing to deal with as a doctor is the rage that some patients feel and can at times project upon the doctor when treating impotence.

After the appearance of Viagra, types or groups of patients are still discussed in association with ED in *Läkartidningen*, but usually these are connected to individuals who have diseases whose symptoms can include, or whose treatments can induce, impotence, that is diabetes, multiple sclerosis, anxiety attacks and heart disease. Thus patients are distinguished into categories based on medical diseases rather than social factors. This later discussion of the types of ED patients in *Läkartidningen* was probably triggered by the debates raging after the introduction of Viagra over who should receive subsidies for the prescriptions of Viagra (see Landtblom and Ertzgaard 2000; Örn 2001). Using Viagra in these cases is presented as a solution to ED for patients with a legitimate need for the drug. I use the word *legitimate* because it is in these cases that the Swedish courts have heard arguments for and against the subsidized use of Viagra as a treatment for severe ED (see Chapter 2).

Sexual problems and pharmaceuticals

From their studies of US cases, sociologists Mamo and Fishman note that prescribing drugs like Viagra can, in some cases, lead to and justify polypharmica (Mamo and Fishman 2001, 27). *Läkartidningen* takes up the occurrence of polypharmica as well. Three years before the introduction of Viagra, the discussion of sexual difficulties and pharmaceuticals was raised in *Läkartidningen* in an article called 'Sex life and pharmaceuticals' (Lundberg 1995). In it, Lundberg discusses both how pharmaceuticals have been developed to treat sexual problems, and how pharmaceuticals taken for other reasons can influence one's sex life. Thus, by 1995, pharmacological sources of, and solutions to, sexual problems were gaining acceptance within the Swedish medical community. But it also shows that the understanding of the concept of sexual problems was very broad before Viagra. In this article, a great deal of time is spent discussing the influence of other drugs (i.e. dopamine and serotonin blockers) on desire rather than on the mechanical ability to have sex, for both men and women. Most interesting, however, is the way sex is defined more widely than it often is in post-Viagra discussions. For example, sex is presented as involving not just intercourse but also orgasms, even for women. And after noting that serotonin blockers can make orgasm difficult for women, the author states, 'There are, however, few reports of orgasm difficulties in men using this type of antidepressant. We do not know if there is a sex-specific difference or if the problem is hidden in men because of the difficulties in differentiating between ejaculation and orgasm' (Lundberg 1995, 2745). The idea that men could experience ejaculation without orgasm is completely absent from any later discussions of Viagra, as is the possibility of having an erection without ejaculation. But in the 1995 article, a nuanced way of discussing pharmaceuticals and sexual health is presented, one that involves desire, ability and pleasure. Much of this nuance is lost with the arrival of Viagra, and discussions about libido and desire also tend to disappear in the literature about ED, in *Läkartidningen* and other medical journals, despite the fact that the makers of Viagra insist that it will not produce an erection without sexual stimulation. But, as many social scientists and critics have noted about Viagra in general, it relies on the traditional understanding of male sexuality, that men *always* want sex (see Fishman and Mamo 2001, 183; Mamo and Fishman 2001, 23; Marshall 2002, 2006; Loe 2004b; Tiefer 2006).

Returning to the discourse in *Läkartidningen*, libido appears only in connection with impotence post-Viagra in two articles. One is the 2004 column 'Pharmaceutical questions' (Kimland and Ståhle 2004), which is a brief compilation of topics discussed at regional pharmaceutical information centres. There, in 2004, the terms *libido* and *impotence* appear together when reporting a study that examined these in connection with the use of lithium (as the 1995 Lundberg article did when talking about sexual problems and pharmaceuticals). The other is a 2008 article that discusses the benefits of off-label use of Sildenafil for women suffering from sexual dysfunction as a result of antidepressants (Bodlund 2008). But these two articles can be read as special cases dealing with the effects of psycho-pharmaceuticals rather than the use of Viagra for a wider population.

Pharmaceuticals and erectile dysfunction

Pharmaceutical solutions for impotence existed prior to Viagra's arrival in 1998, although most of these involved needles or pellets inserted directly into the penis and were therefore not as easy to administer as a pill. However, in a *Läkartidningen* article from 1997 (Hedelin and Abramsson), the use of orally ingested medicines for erectile dysfunction is discussed and their pending introduction to the market predicted. In this article, the term *erectile dysfunction*,[6] rather than *impotence*, is first used in *Läkartidningen*.[7] With this term, the discussion is shifted to the mechanical aspects of blood flow, vascular systems and muscle cells. Men have 'erectile difficulties' and these can be treated. The authors start the article with the statement, 'The ability for a man to have an erection that facilitates intercourse and insemination is a prerequisite for the continuation of the human race' (Hedelin and Abramsson 1997, 2548), and then go on to discuss various possibilities for treatment to be subsidized by the Swedish state, a discussion that later takes on enormous proportions in *Läkartidningen* (Hedelin 1998; Sjöstrand 1998; Beerman 2000; Byström 2000a, 2000b; Landtblom and Ertzgaard 2000; Landtblom 2004; Ströberg *et al.* 2006).

In 1998, Viagra appears in *Läkartidningen*, with articles about the drug itself and about the way it is being received in the United States (Bergström 1998; Branke 1998), its introduction to Sweden, specifics of its use, questions of its costs to the individual and society (Hedelin 1998) and warnings that it is being sold illegally through the mail (Aldstedt 1998). It is at this point that impotence, which in the 1990 and 1995 articles was broadly defined, often with social causes, and which occurred in many different types of patients, including couples, is now directly equated with ED. In the introduction to his 1998 article 'New treatment for impotence', aforementioned urologist Hans Hedelin articulates this discursive coupling: 'Erectile dysfunction (impotence), that is the inability to achieve and maintain an erection for a sufficiently long period for sexual activity, is the most common form of sexual functioning problems' (Hedelin 1998, 4558).

To better contextualize his use of the term *erectile dysfunction*, it is important to note that the discursive sliding between, and in some cases conflation of, impotence and ED has a history outside of the Swedish context, largely in the field of urology and closely connected to the development of pharmaceutical therapies. Social scientist Barbara Marshall, in her work on Viagra, relays the story of how Dr Giles Brindley in 1983, in front of an audience of medical peers, injected his penis with phenoxybenzamine and obtained an erection, essentially removing the connection between emotional or tactile stimulation and erection. Ten years later, in 1993, the US National Institute of Health created consensus around the use of the term *erectile dysfunction* (Marshall 2002, 136). In Sweden, in the 1998 Hedelin article, erectile dysfunction becomes equated with impotence in *Läkartidningen*.

Susan Bordo claims that impotence as a term reflects a characteristic of the person, not a disease – one says of a man, 'he is impotent' while one would not say 'he is a headache' (Bordo 1998, 87). And, as Loe (2004a) has noted, the shift in English from impotence to ED can be quite comfortable for the individual. ED allows the man to maintain his identity and self untainted, and treat only the penis. Potts notes this as well: 'This term [impotence] infers that a man loses power through his "failure" to achieve an erection, and demonstrates how important a notion of "potency" is in constructions of conventional masculine sexuality. Consequently, an inability to produce erections may be perceived as tantamount to a destruction of the male self' (Potts 2004, 23). With the introduction of ED and Viagra, a medical term and a pill exist that can prevent damage to the individual and erase blame for the failure to produce an erection on demand. These comments on terminology are also applicable to the Swedish usages of *impotence* and *erectile dysfunction*.

Another interesting observation in connection with the use of the term *erectile dysfunction* is that, in the 1998 *Läkartidningen* article, Hedelin asserts that ED is 'the most common form of sexual function problems' around the world. This statement was very common in 1998, internationally. That ED became the most common form of sexual function problem just when a medicine to cure it was introduced has been discussed elsewhere in relation to medicalization, biomedicalization and pharmaceuticalization (Mamo and Fishman 2001, 16; Elliott 2003; Loe 2004a; Moynihan and Cassels 2005; Williams *et al.* 2011a). In *Läkartidningen*, articles after 1998 spend a great deal of time talking about the physiology of erections and their molecular and biological aspects, and very little, if any time discussing counselling, couples therapy and the social or relationship issues related to impotence.

Perhaps most indicative of the direction articles about impotence and ED in *Läkartidningen* took after the introduction of Viagra is the 2000 article 'Viagra is the first option for treating erectile dysfunction,' co-authored by urologist Hans Hedelin (who defined erectile dysfunction as impotence) and Pfizer employee Lena Jacobsson. In this article they discuss a study which compared treatments for ED in Sweden. Gone from this study are all questions about the emotional or social aspects of impotence, or even the fact that sexual problems can take other forms than ED. Instead the study only focuses on how ED can be treated pharmacologically. The authors start their article by stating, 'In the last few years different methods to successfully treat erectile dysfunction (ED) have appeared, methods which work largely unrelated to the cause of the erectile problems and which demand a minimum of evaluation before the treatment can be initiated' (Hedelin and Jacobsson 2000, 2616). Thus, the treatment for ED (which impotence had become) is suddenly a relatively simple procedure, rather than one which, as suggested in a 1995 article, demands an empathetic doctor who can give hope and understanding, and who can spend sufficient time with the patient to discuss his/their problems, often over a period of several consultations (Olsson *et al.* 1995, 313). Likewise, in articles appearing prior to Viagra, references to alternative treatments like self-injections to the penis and the use of penis pumps and surgical implants appear, often as later-stage complements to couples therapy (see Olsson *et al.* 1995). This is particularly true with the penis implant, which is discussed with the warning:

> Those patients who expect that an implant will not only create erections but also improve their relationship with their partner and bring them closer to a harmonic life are often disappointed.
>
> (Olsson *et al.* 1995, 316)

However, this is exactly what Viagra promises, as noted in a 1998 *Läkartidningen* article, which argues for subsidies for Viagra because its use cures two patients, not just one, that is also the partner of the man suffering from ED (Sjöstrand 1998). Potts and colleagues (2006) have shown how this idea is also prevalent in English-language commercials for Viagra, and the partner in the Swedish commercial discourse is discussed in Chapter 6.

The shift in the use of the term *impotence* to *erectile dysfunction* occurs in *Läkartidningen* and the post-Viagra articles written largely by urologists, and is not unique to the Swedish discourse. It is in line with what has occurred in other journals and media outlets internationally. As Tiefer notes in her critique of the English-language use of the term, 'erectile dysfunction, a condition in the man's genitalia, has become the only acknowledged focus of interest, focus of evaluation, and focus of treatment. This represents a substantial narrowing from sex therapy – erasing the partner, erasing subjective meaning, and, ironically, perpetuating the obsession with penile hardness, which many sex therapists have argued is itself a primary cause of sexual unhappiness' (Tiefer 2000, 278).

Examples of the same refocusing of the discourse in Sweden can be seen in *Läkartidningen*. Prior to Viagra, mention is made of another closely related sexual problem: premature ejaculation (Olsson *et al.* 1990). But after Viagra, this problem is not discussed again in connection with sexual difficulties until 2006, when a notice about a new drug treatment is presented (Hansen 2006) which mentions that 20–30% of men suffer from premature ejaculation. (Compare with the pre-Viagra book review that states an estimated 10% of men suffer from impotence (Mellgren 1993).) This seems to confirm Marshall's assertion, drawn from her analysis of English-language articles about Viagra, that 'even though premature ejaculation (an "orgasmic disorder") has higher prevalence rates than "erectile dysfunction" in many studies, we do not hear of an "epidemic" of premature ejaculation' (Marshall 2002, 137). Viagra has shifted the focus onto ED, and redirected attention away from other sexual difficulties, including early ejaculation and a lack of libido, internationally and also in the Swedish medical discourse.

The impotent man, the partner patient and a woman's responsibility

Before Viagra, in several of the *Läkartidningen* articles about impotence, the patient is presented as the partner unit. For example, in an article from 1995, the roles of each partner in dealing with impotence are narrowly defined. 'Conversation with the couple is the most important diagnostic and therapeutic instrument. One should strive to work with the couple rather than the man alone, though one should never try to force the partner's cooperation. Men and women have different ways of expressing themselves and therefore misunderstandings can easily arise. Women must learn to be clearer and men to be more receptive' (Olsson *et al.* 1995, 313). In addition to charging each partner with a specific way of communicating and the responsibility to change this, the article notes: 'The best help for a man with disappointing erections is, besides his own courage to speak about it, an understanding and sensual partner who is sexually keen but not demanding' (Olsson *et al.* 1995, 314). Although, as the authors go on to say, 'of course, this isn't always enough' (Olsson *et al.* 1995, 314).

The couple-patient is also present when talking about other sexual problems pre-Viagra, as here, when discussing early ejaculation: 'Naturally, the sexual act can easily be a failure in these situations unless the female partner is wise and possibly experienced, and can focus primary attention on physical contact and intimacy, and reduce the importance of genital contact' (Olsson *et al.* 1990, 4456). The woman is charged with responsibility for ensuring that the sexual act is a success, despite the man's sexual problems. This is slightly different than when speaking about impotence as a partner issue or presenting the impotent patient as a partner constellation. Instead, the solution to the sexual problem is in the hands of the female partner. This same shift of responsibility for curing the patient occurs in the discussion about (male) libido. When expanding on the difference between desire and libido, and their relationship to impotence, the authors state that, 'Naturally, even here the female partner's behaviour is very important' (Olsson *et al.* 1990, 4456). Also of note is the distinct sense that impotence occurs only in heterosexual relations. And, as the earlier discussion about men and women's communication issues implies, not only is the patient a heterosexual couple, it is a couple with very stereotypical, gender-specific interaction patterns.

In 1998, after the introduction of Viagra, the definition of the patient with ED shifts from the couple to the man in *Läkartidningen*. The only articles which suggest the presence of a female Viagra patient is the aforementioned 1998 article which argues that the debate about whether to subsidize Viagra should take into consideration that the pill helps two patients, not one (Sjöstrand 1998) and the 2008 article about using Viagra for women on antidepressants (Bodlund 2008).[8] Other than these, however, the post-Viagra ED patient is primarily the man prescribed the pills, and often only the genitals of that man.

The assumption of heterosexual patients in the Swedish case is not unique and mirrors a wider heteronormativity in the English-language discussions about Viagra and impotence, this despite the widespread use of Viagra within homosexual communities, and despite the use of the gender-neutral term *partner* in Pfizer advertising (see Chapter 6). For further discussion, see McLaren (2007) and Vares and Braun (2006).

Reopening the debate

Not until 2006 does the partner-patient unit of ED appear again in the post-Viagra *Läkartidningen.* In this year the partner becomes one of the people who should be asked about evaluation of the treatment and one of the reasons patients chose to discontinue treatment (Ströberg *et al.* 2006, 1107). While the integration of the partner in the discourse can be related to his/her presence in the pre-Viagra articles, this is a somewhat new role for the partner. Rather than being part of the cure, as in the articles from the early 1990s, now the partner is part of the wider context that influences a patient's decision to follow a medical cure. It is also in this 2006 article that the social factors behind ED are finally reintroduced to the discourse, after having been absent for eight years. In the discussion about the discontinuation of pharmaceutical treatments for ED, the results of the Pfizer-funded study showed that more than half of the patients prescribed Sildenafil stopped using it within two years. To explain this, the authors report that 'Often the reasons are multi-factoral and factors like increasing age, diminished libido, relationship problems, health problems, social and cultural background all together can influence the decision to stop treatment' (Ströberg *et al.* 2006, 2866). Issues concerning the physiology of ED were not the only, or even primary, answers they received from patients. This article in *Läkartidningen* shows that when a study is conducted which actually asks Viagra patients about their experiences and the reasons for their use or disuse of the drug, a disjuncture of the drug's patients and their medically prescribed sexual identities and practices begins to (re)appear.

That international medical research about the use of pharmaceutical treatments for ED is focused on biological, mechanical or molecular aspects of erections has been noted. As Tiefer wrote in 2000, 'There's little attention to the person or couple attached to the penis, or recognition that relational factors might modify the meaning or importance of penile rigidity or sexual intercourse in a couple's sexual script. It would appear that industry-sponsored research wishes simply to wave away the complexities introduced by the psychosocial context of sexuality' (Tiefer 2000, 278). As an example of pharmaceuticalization, the case of Viagra in Sweden before the 2006 study complicates the medicalization hypothesis that general medicine is trying to constantly expand the domain over which it reigns. The examples of medical intervention for impotence in the pre-Viagra articles in *Läkartidningen* suggest that doctors were willing to intervene in the biomedical and social aspects of their patients' sexuality, but that after Viagra's appearance, medical intervention is narrowed to the biomechanical functions of a man's penis. This narrowing runs counter to some expected processes of medicalization, but shows how pharmaceuticalization tries to confine the condition of impotence to one disease (ED) with a universal, pharmaceutical treatment.

This tendency makes the Pfizer-funded Ströberg, Hedelin and Bergström (2006) study in *Läkartidningen* even more noteworthy, as it perhaps suggests that Viagra has not successfully reduced impotence to ED. Their article reopens the discussion of factors that can influence sexual health and simultaneously remedicalizes the larger context of patients' sexual health. One could have hoped that this signalled a return to a more nuanced discussion of sexual problems and their treatments within *Läkartidningen* and that acknowledging that there may be diverse reasons for patients to discontinue treatment with Viagra and similar medications may lead the medical discourse to include aspects from the early 1990s, that is recognition that there are different types of patients who have different reasons for and understandings of their impotence, along with the existence of a pill. By comparison, it is relatively uncomplicated to assert that women's sexualities are complex and context dependent, and that they are influenced by feelings and emotions, even with older women (see, for example, Loe's (2004b) study). One could have hoped that the 2006 article in *Läkartidningen* was a sign that soon Swedish men, too, would be granted the right to (once again) own a complicated and context-dependent sexuality influenced by feelings, emotions and social situations, not just kicked into action with a drug. But in the years that followed, little seemed to change. Viagra continued to be discussed in articles about subsidies and in relation to other medical conditions, like cardiovascular and prostate problems. Thus, in the Swedish medical discourse, the local structures doctors and health care providers worked in combined with Viagra's global traits to create a glocal Viagra in *Läkartidningen*, one which presented and maintained a pharmaceutical solution to erectile dysfunction.

Notes

1 An earlier version of this chapter has been published as Johnson, E. (2008). Chemistries of Love: Impotence, Erectile Dysfunction and Viagra in *Läkartidningen*, *NORMA, 3* (1), 31–47.

2 *Läkartidningen* is the trade journal of the Swedish Medical Association (*Läkarförbund*). It is published about once a week and covers international and Swedish developments in medicine and medical care.

3 In Swedish: *Impotens, impotensmedel, peniserektion, erektil dysfunktion, erektil svårigheter, potensmedel, Viagra, Sildenafil.*

4 All translations are the author's.

5 www.viagra.se (October 2015).

6 Much later, in 2005, an interesting shift is made when erectile dysfunction, which had been a side effect of some diseases, also becomes a symptom. *Läkartidningen* reported that erectile dysfunction may be a symptom of undiagnosed heart disease and encouraged doctors who have a patient with ED to find out if that patient actually has heart disease (Gunnarsdottar 2005).

7 Masters and Johnson used the term *erectile dysfunction* in the 1950s (McLaren 2007, 221). However, it was generally not taken up by the medical community until adopted by urologists and popularized by Pfizer (see Marshall 2002; Loe 2004a).

8 See Loe (2004b) for an analysis of senior women in the United States and the drug.

5 Alpha-blockers and a weaker pharmaceutical influence on medical discourse

Ericka Johnson

As Illich pointed out many years ago, a drug's commercial and medical success is not terribly dependent on its chemical effects on the body (Illich 1976, 72). This observation has given impetus to critical work on pharmaceuticals that explores factors which make drugs as varied as Viagra, antidepressants and Botox so successful (Fishman and Mamo 2001; Elliot 2003; Moynihan and Cassels 2005; Marshall 2006; Petryna and Kleinman 2006), and spawned studies of the way pharmaceuticalization influences medical and social practices (Williams *et al.* 2011a). In this body of work it becomes clear that one important factor, among many, that can impact a drug's success is the way it is constructed and situated in the professional medical discourse and the medical infrastructure of a specific country, a trait pharmaceuticals share with many other medical technologies (see Healy 2000; Löwy 2015).

This section of this book explores local examples of a pharmaceutical's ability to influence the treatment of established medical conditions and redefine health problems as issues with a pharmaceutical solution. The previous chapter explored the influence Viagra had on the medical discourse in Sweden. In this chapter, I am again relying on an analysis of the medical discourse in the Swedish-language medical journal *Läkartidningen*. From it, I have retrieved research articles and debate pages that appear when the journal's online archive is searched for the Swedish words associated with lower urinary tract symptoms secondary to benign prostate hyperplasia (LUTS/BPH): BPH, *prostatahyperplasi* and *prostatahypertrofi*.[1] I have conducted a search for the years between 1990 and 2015, since alpha-blockers started to become a more common treatment method in Europe for LUTS/BPH in the 1990s (EUA 2006, 35) and were registered as a treatment for BPH in Sweden in the early 1990s (Carlsson and Spångberg 1996a, 4549; Hallin 1999, 3520). This time frame mirrors that used for Viagra in the previous chapter.

Alpha-blockers are an interesting case for a book about glocal pharmaceuticalization because they show an example of incomplete change in the medical discourse and clinical practice for the treatment of LUTS/BPH, as opposed to Viagra, which completely changed the face of a disease and its treatment. Alpha-blockers are also related to an analysis of Viagra because one of their side effects is impotence and/or erectile dysfunction. Medical guidelines suggest that men taking alpha-blockers may experience decreased desire and erectile and ejaculatory difficulties (EAU 2006; AUA 2010; SBU 2011). Many men who receive a prescription for alpha-blockers will also receive a prescription for Viagra, although probably to very limited success, given that Viagra does not address desire.

Alpha-blockers are being prescribed to treat LUTS/BPH in Sweden as in other developed, Western countries. In fact, some Swedish experts assert that they are being overprescribed. Yet, despite their presence in the Swedish cadre of treatments for close to twenty-five years, and despite their place as an early course of action for LUTS/BPH, according to an official Swedish diagnostic and treatment report (SBU 2011), they have not managed to replace surgical treatments as completely as Viagra managed to replace sex therapists in the *Läkartidningen* discourse or out in the urology clinics. By the early 2000s, 40,000 men were being treated pharmaceutically for BPH in Sweden (Dahlstrand 2003, 2678), and by 2009, this number had risen to approximately 115,000 (Spångberg and Dahlgren 2013, 685), a significant increase, even if one considers the possibility that pharmaceutical treatments also increased the gross number of patients diagnosed with LUTS/BPH. At the same time, surgical procedures had declined, but were still relatively high. In 1987, before alpha-blockers, 12,000 surgeries for enlarged prostates were performed in Sweden. In 2009, just under 5,000 were performed (Spångberg and Dahlgren 2013, 685). This is a decrease, but shows that surgery is still the treatment option for thousands of Swedish men each year and is still presented as an option in the discourse in *Läkartidningen.*

LUTS/BPH and alpha-blockers

The search terms I used for this study are the Swedish words which are or have recently been applied to what is today known as LUTS/BPH, lower urinary tract symptoms secondary to benign prostate hyperplasia in English. This is a condition in which the prostate becomes enlarged but without being cancerous. The prostate can start to grow again in older men, gradually increasing in size with age, and this is thought to happen in the majority of men. For some, it happens around age fifty, for others, not until they are seventy or older. It is a normal development, but this normal growth can cause problems with urination and is thus considered pathological. By the age of seventy, 75% of men will have LUTS/BPH symptoms, that is problems urinating (Parsons 2007, 395), and by age eighty, nearly all men will have an enlarged prostate (Fall 1999, 2227), 80% of whom will have problems with urination (Dahlstrand 2003, 2678). These statistics tend to vary a bit, but the general understanding is that the prostate gets larger as men get older, and that causes problems urinating.

Urologists like to point out that urination issues for men have existed for thousands of years, referring to drawings on Egyptian papyrus from the fifteenth century BC and to writings by Hippocrates (Shackley 1999, 776). Medically, however, the prostate as a separate organ was not represented in European anatomy diagrams until 1536, and not named until 1611 (Marx and Karenberg 2009, 209). Successful methods of surgically addressing the prostate for urination difficulties did not really evolve until just more than 100 years ago (Shackley 1999,

776). Today, a connection is often made between male urinary problems and an enlarged prostate. It is thought that when the prostate gets larger it may also start to block the urethra, the tube that lets the urine pass from the bladder and which the prostate surrounds, like a straw stuck through a ball. When the prostate begins to block the flow of urine through the urethra, its enlargement becomes a problem.

The first step of treatment for LUTS/BPH is currently pharmaceutical. This is a relatively recent change and it has complemented but not entirely replaced the traditionally more common surgery. Around the turn of the twentieth century, surgeries were performed for prostate issues, but with very high risks primarily due to infection. These surgeries would access the prostate from the abdomen or, more commonly, through a Y-shaped incision behind the testicles. These days, the LUTS/BPH prostate is usually surgically accessed through the urethra and the most common method is by transurethral resection of the prostate (TURP), which sends a tool in through the urethra to scrape away and cauterize the prostate tissue from the inside (AUA 2010, 70). There are other mechanical ways of removing or destroying a prostate diagnosed with LUTS/BPH, including microwave thermotherapy, radiofrequency needle ablation and laser therapies, but besides pharmaceuticals, surgery is the most common method in Sweden (SBU 2011).

Pharmaceutical treatment can be traced to the introduction of alpha-blockers in the 1970s (Heyns and de Klerk 1989, 226) and their eventual position as a standard treatment starting in the 1990s. However, even before alpha-blockers, LUTS/BPH had been treated by suppositories, herbal treatment, chemicals and hormones. Chemical preparations doctors historically prescribed for patients include opium, silver nitrate and belladonna suppositories, potassium iodine, potassium bromide, ergot (a type of fungi that grows on rye) and large quantities of distilled water (Marting 1903, 52; O'Shea 2012, 14). Many of these treatments were directed at the symptoms the man presented with, primarily urination problems, and some of the elixirs irrigated the bladder, but others, like ergot, were actually thought to shrink the prostate gland (O'Shea 2012, 14).

At the end of the nineteenth century, it was generally thought that 'orchidectomy' (surgically removing one or both of the testicles) and vasectomy could be two treatments for the enlarged prostate that may have beneficial effects (Heyns and de Klerk 1989, 204; Shackley 1999, 777). This theory was in part developed because the then-current surgical methods (primarily suprapubic prostatectomy) had a mortality rate of about 20%, so other treatment methods were very welcome by patients and doctors alike. But the ideas about using castration and vasectomy could also be traced to the observation that eunuchs and those with non-developed testicles never presented with 'hypertrophy' of the prostate (Ciechanowski 1903, 91), indicating that the testes were somehow involved in the development of prostate growth later in life. While clinical practice did not really support the use of castration for treatment – many doctors reported that it was not successful and that patients were not pleased with the results (Marting 1903) – the possibility that it could work eventually led to theories about the role of hormones in prostate enlargement. However, it took until sometime into the twentieth century before hormone therapies were widely developed and used for prostate issues (O'Shea

2012, 17; see also Oudshoorn 1994, 2003 and Sengoopta 2006 for general histories of hormone treatments and their relationship to masculinity). In the 1930s and 1940s, androgens, especially testosterone, were used to treat patients with what was then called 'prostatism', but without much success. The next step was to try oestrogen and combinations of oestrogen and testosterone. This did not really work to reduce the prostate, either, although it did seem to give some relief of symptoms and increase urine flow (Heyns and de Klerk 1989, 221). In the 1970s and 1980s a series of trials were done on antiandrogens and progestins. Some of these showed symptom improvement and others did not, and many of the trials had quite a few side effects, like vertigo, shivering, tiredness, loss of libido and impotence (Heyns and de Klerk 1989, 221–3). Cholesterol-lowering drugs were also tested, but with no significant benefit (Heyns and de Klerk 1989, 23–4).

At the same time, in the 1970s and 1980s, doctors also began to try alpha-blockers, with more success. They seemed better than placebos at treating peak and average flow rates of urination, the amounts of residual urine and even the prostatic urethral pressure (Heyns and de Klerk 1989, 226), so much so that it has been suggested that their relative success may also have increased the interest in diagnosing LUTS/BPH (Ekman 1999, 3504). It is this category of drugs, alpha-blockers, that I will explore in the Swedish medical literature.

Alpha-blockers

Alpha-blockers' main purpose as a treatment for LUTS/BPH is to reduce the symptoms and bother of urination problems (SBU 2011, 317), and their use has steadily increased since the 1990s, probably in part because patients (and their doctors) see them as a way of avoiding surgery and in part because of increased marketing from pharmaceutical companies (EUA 2006, 35).

Alpha-blockers work on the smooth muscle tissue of the prostate. One theory about the cause of LUTS/BPH is that, as the prostate increases in size, the increase in prostatic smooth muscle tissue interferes with urethral constriction and impairs the flow of urine (AUA 2010, 13). Reducing this process and changing the behaviour of the smooth muscle cells by ingesting alpha-blockers can then help to relieve the blockage and enable better urination. However, alpha-blockers, which are ingested orally, do not only work on the muscle cells of the prostate; they can affect smooth muscle cells all over the body, which leads to side effects like headaches, dizziness, hypertension, retrograde ejaculation and, as mentioned earlier, sometimes erectile dysfunction. Newer versions of alpha-blockers, which are better at targeting the prostate specifically, are being developed and marketed, but for the most part, treatment with alpha-blockers is followed by various side effects.

If alpha-blockers are going to work for a man, he should notice a difference relatively quickly, some within forty-eight hours, and no longer than a month after beginning treatment (EUA 2006, 36). Different ways of measuring the results of treatment are commonly used to determine if alpha-blockers are effective, including reiterations of the symptom scale questionnaire, pressure, flow and volume measures and by measuring the volume of the prostate, to see if it has shrunk at all. A third of men will not notice any symptom improvement at all (EUA 2006, 36) and, according to Swedish pharmaceutical registry statistics, two-thirds of the men will stop taking alpha-blockers within three years (Spångberg and Dahlgren 2013, 685). If they do work, the patient can continue taking the alpha-blockers for the rest of his life.

Thus, the actual success of treating LUTS/BPH with alpha-blockers is contested. The American Urology Association (AUA) says that alpha-blockers 'produce significant symptom improvement compared to placebo that the average patient will appreciate as a moderate improvement from baseline' (AUA 2010, 28). But what is significant is a matter of debate. In the national Swedish report for treatment of LUTS/BPH done by the Swedish Agency for Health Technology Assessment, alpha-blockers are said to reduce the symptom bother slightly and increase the flow rate slightly better than placebos (SBU 2011, 321). The results are statistically significant but rather small (SBU 2011, 335). As the European Association of Urology (EAU) guidelines suggest, there are very real placebo effects to take into consideration (EAU 2006, 35) and, as the SBU overview noted, there is always a publication bias to statistical evaluations based on published studies; unsuccessful studies do not tend to be published. Of all the published studies that the SBU found to evaluate, none had been financed by independent sources; all were funded by the pharmaceutical industry (SBU 2011, 317–18). They suggest that it is important to remember that scientific and commercial interests have influenced the design, conduct and evaluation of the studies on which conclusions about alpha-blockers are based (SBU 2011, 325). My analysis of the medical discourse in *Läkartidningen* would suggest that resource distribution and professional hierarchies implicit in the structural organization of professional health care in Sweden are also relevant factors in the moderate success of alpha-blockers within the process of pharmaceuticalization of LUTS/BPH. They are not the only factors, but they are involved.

Alpha-blockers for LUTS/BPH in *Läkartidningen*

Treatment for LUTS/BPH in Sweden can take one of three paths – and sometimes all three through the course of the disease. One can engage in 'watchful waiting', which means the patient is sent home and told to keep an eye on things and come back if his urination problems become more serious. If the patient is already so bothered by his LUTS/BPH that watchful waiting is not an option, the treatment can either be lifelong medication, beginning with the use of alpha-blockers, potentially combined with 5-Alpha-reductase inhibitors (5-ARIs), or the problem can be addressed surgically or through other means of removing or destroying the prostate. (There are natural dietary supplements, herbal medicines and exercise programmes which are also said to help, but these are not covered by the urology-dominated discourse in *Läkartidningen*.)

Alpha-blockers could have been a game changer for the treatment of LUTS/BPH when they were introduced in the 1990s. And to some extent, they have been, but not entirely. When they started being used, the main treatment for severe

BPH was surgery. The surgical removal of parts of the prostate through the urethra has been in general use in Sweden since the end of the 1960s (Hedelin *et al.* 2003, 2441). However, the introduction of alpha-blockers has not removed surgery as an option for treatment, even if the official diagnostic and treatment overview (SBU 2011) suggests that alpha-blockers are a first-step treatment, to be tried before surgical removal or reduction of the prostate. Yet surgery for an enlarged prostate and the urination problems it is thought to cause is still a very widely used method in Sweden (and in other countries), and the surgical techniques are continually being advanced technically, with hospitals purchasing expensive robotic surgery systems, partly as recruitment tools to attract urology surgeons (Lindgren 1999), and TURP simulators for training purposes are being developed and used (Källström 2010). The most recent articles in *Läkartidningen* mention both surgery and pharmaceutical treatments on equal grounds (Degerblad *et al.* 2014). So, as an example of pharmaceuticals changing the treatment practices of already medicalized diseases, alpha-blockers are only partially successful.

When they arrived on the scene, alpha-blockers did not have to do any convincing about the 'realness' of LUTS/BPH or its presence in the enlarged prostate diagnosis. Problems with urination had already been accepted, both the legitimacy of patient suffering and the legitimacy of paying for treatment with tax money in Sweden. LUTS/BPH was an established disease with established treatments that were costly and that cost was not controversial. What was controversial in the Swedish medical discourse was shifting that cost from surgery provision to pharmaceutical distribution. In 1996, an article about new, expensive pharmaceuticals for urological treatments, written by a leading urologist, compared their increasing costs (and potential share of a limited health care budget) with the cost of more traditional urology care, claiming that the increased costs for medicines for prostate cancer, BPH and erectile dysfunction 'would equal the annual costs of running between five and six medium sized urology clinics'[2] (Carlsson and Spångberg 1996a, 4552). In this argument the cost of medication is directly compared to the cost of funding clinical treatments in urology. Resources for drugs are rhetorically placed in direct competition with urologists' salaries and clinical costs.

The concern about cost is particularly relevant to the local context of alpha-blockers in Sweden, reflecting both the tax-based structure of health care funding in Sweden and the fact that LUTS/BPH treatments are accessed within a health care system that has designated specialists – urologists – who treat LUTS/BPH and gatekeepers to those specialists, general practitioners. With alpha-blockers, there was debate and concern about cost in general, although the concern seems to be more related to the fact that use of alpha-blockers for the treatment of LUTS/BPH is a lifelong medication, whereas the (arguably expensive) surgery it is sometimes thought to replace is a one-off cost (Hedelin *et al.* 2001, 2441). However, in the debate about whether to treat with alpha-blockers or to treat with surgery also lurked an implication of which type of doctor was allowed to treat LUTS/BPH and where the state resources for it would then go. In Sweden, a man with suspected LUTS/BPH cannot make an appointment with an urologist on his own;

he must receive a referral to the urology specialist from his general practitioner. General practitioners are not allowed to conduct TURP surgeries, but they can – at least theoretically – prescribe alpha-blockers (Hassler 2002, 2174). By shifting the first line of treatment to alpha-blockers, there is the potential that LUTS/BPH patients will become a case for general practitioners but not urologists. To some extent this has happened, but not entirely, and here, too the medical discourse has focused on how alpha-blockers can potentially shift cost and resource distribution within the health care system (Carlsson and Spångberg 1996b, 4557). In the early 2000s, it was estimated that one in four patients was beginning treatment with alpha-blockers or other pharmaceuticals before visiting a urologist (Hedelin *et al.* 2003, 1435). This does not mean that urologists have lost 25% of their LUTS/BPH patients – on the contrary. There has been a dramatic rise in the number of patients presenting with LUTS/BPH since the early 1990s, probably due to the existence of alpha-blockers and their use as a treatment at an earlier stage in the disease. But nonetheless, the discourse in *Läkartidningen* shows a concern about patients being treated outside of, and prior to, consultation with a urology specialist, despite that the Swedish urology field is currently understaffed and there are long waiting lists for meeting a urologist, as the field is very occupied with prostate cancer.

For the treatment of LUTS/BPH, a shift from being a disease treated by specialists to one managed by general practitioners can also carry with it a step down the prestige ladder (see Witz 1992; Lindgren 1999), and one which could mean a transfer of resources from the more prestigious speciality (urology) to the less prestigious world of general practitioners, as the comparison of increasing costs of pharmaceutical treatments to clinic costs could suggest. This competition between GPs and urologists has been articulated elsewhere, like in the debate about whose finger is better at conducting the digital rectal exam of the prostate, the general practitioner's or the urologist's (see Kirby *et al.* 1995). It may have had an influence on the extent to which alpha-blockers replaced surgery in the Swedish context.

The final words in the debate between alpha-blockers and surgical treatments for LUTS/BPH may yet remain to be written. One of the urologists I interviewed suggested that the new framing of BPH as primarily LUTS in the 2013 European Association of Urology clinical guidelines (Oelke *et al.* 2013) is a result of alpha-blockers – or lobbying by their producers and supporters – to change the focus from the enlarged prostate to the lower urinary tract symptoms and thereby shift the focus from potentially removing an enlarged gland and instead treating the muscles in and around it with pharmaceuticals.

More recently, there has been little debate about the use of alpha-blockers in *Läkartidningen*, which would suggest that the usage has stabilized. Alpha-blockers' place in treatment practice has also been formalized in the 2011 overview published by the Swedish Agency for Health Technology Assessment. The chair of the committee who authored this report is the same urologist who raised the comparison of costs in relation to urology clinics in 1996, and who wrote a 2013 article in *Läkartidningen* reviewing the overview. His voice, together with the health care policy analysts he co-authored with, raised concerns about the (over) use of alpha-blockers, while simultaneously noting their relatively small success rate (Spångberg and Dahlgren 2013, 683).

Strong and weak pharmaceuticalization: alpha-blockers and Viagra in *Läkartidningen*

As discussed in Chapter 4, Viagra changed the concept of ED and impotence, its treatment and even who its patient was in the Swedish medical discourse, as it did in the international discourse. Yet particularly local Swedish aspects appeared in the discourse around Viagra, related to local (nation state) health care provision specificities, particularly the division of labour between GPs and specialists, and the funding structures for clinical care and pharmaceutical provision. There are some similarities here to what happened with alpha-blockers in the *Läkartidningen* discourse, but also some significant differences.

One similarity between the Viagra discourse and that surrounding the use of alpha-blockers is the concern about cost, yet there are some significant differences between them, too. This was a very heated debate about Viagra, and dealt primarily with the potential costs a state subsidy of the pharmaceutical would entail, an argument that spilled over into the court system, as Chapter 2 detailed. The Viagra cost debate focused on the sheer (potential) cost of the drug for a desiring public and its legitimacy within a tax-funded system, based on the question of whether old-age impotence was a legitimate disease to spend tax resources on. Within the alpha-blocker debate, the question of cost was framed as one of where within the health care system the disease would be treated, and whether resources should be used to support clinics or pharmaceuticals. The legitimacy of spending tax money to treat LUTS/BPH was never questioned.

Viagra also changed the way impotence (now ED) was treated, which alpha-blockers only partially managed to do. Here the most interesting difference with alpha-blockers can be found. Perhaps the incompleteness of the shift from surgery to pharmaceutical treatment is because the representatives of the other method of treatment (surgery) are not from a less prestigious and weaker field of medicine. In the Viagra case, when Viagra was introduced it shifted the event of impotence from a problem for sexual and couples therapists to a disease (ED) under the remit of urologists. The urologists were able to claim this territory from the sex therapists without much visible resistance. However, LUTS/BPH was already a disease of urology when the pharmaceuticals arrived on the scene and despite indications that general practitioners may be beginning to prescribe alpha-blockers for it, urologists are trying to keep LUTS/BPH in their remit. Rather than facilitating a shift from one medical field to another, alpha-blockers merely created two different factions within urology: those who were still using surgery, and those who were willing to treat LUTS/BPH with pharmaceuticals.

Given that the introduction of alpha-blockers could have replaced an expensive, invasive surgical procedure, one could have expected it to cause a change in treatment practices more readily and thoroughly, as Viagra did. But this was not the case. Surgical procedures are down significantly from their occurrence rate before alpha-blockers were officially part of the treatment cadre, but there are still many thousands conducted each year in Sweden. Perhaps one clue to why can be found in the fact that with Viagra there was no actor who/which had traditionally received large resources for the treatment of impotence. Sexual therapists existed (and still exist) in Sweden, but their branch of medicine was peripheral compared to urology, and not nearly as well funded. The occurrence of impotence was medicalized, but its treatment costs were minimal and it was somewhat considered a natural part of getting older that men should just accept (see McLaren 2007). This was not the case with urination problems. The shift of ownership of impotence from sex therapists to urologists that Viagra facilitated was from a low-prestige field to a higher-prestige one. But for alpha-blockers, the potential shift was from a surgical branch of urology to a non-surgical branch of urology. This can either be considered two equal branches in the same field, or envisioned as a shift from a high-prestige to a lower-prestige branch in the same field of medicine, depending on how one sees it (cf. Lindgren 1999). Alpha-blockers were not a tool that could be used to capture the right to diagnose and treat a problem from one specialty to another. Urologists were already conducting surgeries for LUTS/BPH, and it is primarily urologists who are prescribing alpha-blockers. Increasing their use could potentially allow GPs more space in the game, but the urologists seem to be a more powerful voice in the discourse. In fact, no GPs were authoring articles about LUTS/BPH and alpha-blockers in *Läkartidningen* during the period studied, unlike the Viagra discourse, which saw a shift in who was the author of most of these texts. In the alpha-blockers for LUTS/BPH discourse, nearly all of the articles are written by or giving the opinions of urologists – eleven of them – throughout the entire time period searched, with the exception of a few pharmacists and pharmaceutical policy analysts. This is different than the authors, who were given space in the Viagra discussion, where sex therapists and sexologists were writing about impotence before Viagra, and urologists were writing about erectile dysfunction after Viagra's arrival.

The case of alpha-blockers in Sweden can nuance our understanding of pharmaceuticalization by showing that the existence of the drug and its acceptance into the official retinue of treatment options is not enough to predict the success of a new pharmaceutical treatment. Success is also related to which actors (individuals, commercial interests and medical practitioners, a heterogeneous category) use the drugs to make the shifts that occur. Locally, with the case of alpha-blockers in Sweden, the specific concerns with cost and resource distribution related to the government-financed organization of speciality clinics may have impacted the amount of success the alpha-blocker treatment has had in replacing existing therapies, and seems to certainly have influenced the way it was presented in the medical discourse.

Alpha-blockers have become an earlier step in the disease trajectory, a sort of middle stage before eventual treatment with surgery, even though many men are prescribed alpha-blockers with the idea that they will have to take them for the rest of their lives, and may avoid surgery by doing so. The ability of alpha-blockers to shift the treatment paradigm of an existing medical condition from surgery to pharmaceutical has been weaker than that of Viagra. But they have still managed to take over some of the patients and, perhaps more important, they have managed to increase the number of patients identified as having LUTS/BPH. Alpha-blockers have been part of a process of pharmaceuticalization of an existing medical condition, but this process has been only partially successful.

Notes

1 There has been a more recent debate about the dangers of using an anti-inflammatory drug for BPH because of its negative effect on heart patients already taking glucosamine, a debate that has primarily been related to Pfizer's heavy marketing of Artrox, its alleged influence on Swedish safety and side-effect recommendations to doctors, Pfizer's alleged attempts to debunk studies which criticize its effectiveness and safety, and its increased cost, compared to other drugs (see Beermann 2003; Fuberg 2003a, 2003b; Järhult and Lindahl 2003a, 2003b, 2003c; Lohm and Lindh 2003;; Nilsson *et al.* 2003; Lohm *et al.* 2003; Järhult 2005). This is not an alpha-blocker and is therefore not analyzed in this chapter.

2 All translations are the author's.

Part 3

Techno-social relationships and identities

6 Enrolling men, their doctors and partners

Individual and collective responses to erectile dysfunction[1]

Ericka Johnson and Cecilia Åsberg

This chapter examines how men, their doctors and their partners are enrolled by the Pfizer-sponsored website for potential Swedish Viagra customers. We read this enrolment as an example of how new techno-social identities are created by a drug, in this case, Viagra. The Swedish-language site www.potenslinjen.se[2] (in English, 'potency hotline') is framed as a source of information for laypeople concerned about erectile dysfunction.[3] We have examined how the site's text and imagery address different audiences in the construction of the Swedish Viagra man. Our analysis builds on existing literature about the promotion of Viagra which addresses the construction of erectile dysfunction (ED) and masculinity in other national contexts, and we therefore make mention of alternative images and readings in other contexts throughout our analysis. Like previous critical studies of Viagra (Fishman and Mamo 2001; Marshall 2006; Tiefer 2006; Vares and Braun 2006), we are examining the construction of an ideal user of Viagra, but we also discuss the way the enrolment of doctors and partners serves to position ED in the man and define its treatment as a solitary act of taking a pill while simultaneously involving the other actors to help the medicine function.

Our contribution delineates the specific roles the various subjects are granted in the commercial discourse, in particular by looking at the invisible work the 'passive' female partner is tasked with as she is told to actively guide and support her partner in the Viagra trajectory. To think through the creation of the Viagra-specific techno-social identities within the pharmaceuticalization framework (Williams *et al.* 2011a), we use the Actor Network Theory (ANT) concept of enrolment, which articulates the roles given to various actors as they are enrolled into a network that discursively constructs ED as an illness and Viagra as a cure.

The global and the local become relevant in this chapter when the empirical material is read against the framework of regulations regarding DTC marketing of pharmaceuticals. The legality of DTC advertising of prescription pharmaceuticals in the United States and New Zealand has spawned much of the critical research about Viagra and its role in the media climate (see Mamo and Fishman 2001; Elliot 2003; Loe 2004b; Moynihan and Cassels 2005; Potts and Tiefer 2006). And the illegal advertising with near impunity of pharmaceuticals in countries which do ban DTC advertising has been detailed by Zetterqvist and Mulinari (2013) and Zetterqvist and colleagues (2015). Our study, looking at Viagra in the Swedish context, which bans DTC advertising for prescription drugs, confirms the results of much of this work but contributes an important insight to the strength and flexibility of Viagra marketing in a globalized pharmaceutical market. There is a good deal of harmonization between the Swedish site and other Viagra sites, yet also local adaptation (see also Chapter 7). And as we show here, the local adaptation of Viagra marketing that is not considered DTC advertising relies on the construction of subjectivities for the man, his doctor and his partner. The Swedish site is a 'purely informational' site about erectile dysfunction (although it is obviously advertising Viagra) and therefore has information explaining what sex therapy can offer men suffering from impotence in addition to pharmaceutical solutions to ED. The site has previously (2009) listed the telephone number to a sexual medicine centre at a large hospital in Stockholm that receives undirected funds from Pfizer and recently (2015) suggests that men use sexual or psychological therapy for cases when erectile problems have psychological or social causes. In these cases, the site suggests men turn to *The Yellow Pages*. Despite the DTC ban, Viagra figures largely on the website in its colour schemes and Pfizer branding, even if the word *Viagra* is generally absent.

Viagra has figured largely in the 'collective psyche' in Sweden both as a subject of newspaper articles (some reading as if they have been taken directly from drug company PR sheets) and of public debate, thanks in large part to the drawn-out discussions and court cases about whether the Swedish health care system should or would subsidize Viagra (see Chapters 2 and 4). Despite the ban on DTC advertising, a wide range of commercially produced informational material about Viagra is available in Sweden: free pamphlets and booklets which men or their partners can order from Pfizer; literature for doctors and other medical professionals; press coverage in local and national newspapers; informational material on publicly funded webpages about men's health. We have, for this chapter, focused on the website www.potenslinjen.se for a number of reasons: it is produced by Pfizer for a Swedish audience in the Swedish language; it is easily accessible to anyone with an Internet connection and does not require interfacing with a medical practitioner; it focuses on impotence and erectile dysfunction rather than men's health in general; it can be accessed by and addresses individuals not facing impotence personally, like partners and friends. Additionally, the website is a good example of how Pfizer tweaks its material to localize a global message for its global product. Viagra is available in Sweden, but falls outside of the state-subsidized pharmaceutical scheme, which means patients must pay for the drug themselves, creating challenges for marketing the drug. This is addressed by a short film on the website, encouraging men to avoid dangerous, black market purchases and explaining how easy it is to get a prescription and buy the 'real thing' at a drugstore. By analyzing the discourse on www.potenslinjen.se, we argue that the challenge of encouraging men to buy Viagra has been met on the website in part by enrolling men, their doctors and their partners in the ways we detail later in this chapter.

In analyzing the text and images on this site, we have been inspired by the critical studies of Viagra mentioned earlier in this book as well as Foucault's idea of an economy of discourses about sexuality. We are looking at the material presented on the website as an example of an economy of discourses in an attempt to articulate 'the necessities of their operation, the tactics they employ [and] the effects of power which underlie them and which they transmit' (Foucault 1987 [1976], 68f). We also draw inspiration from studies of scientific discourse and naturalized embodiment that feminist scholars have produced since the late 1970s on powerful ideological processes (cf. Merchant 1980; Haraway 1989; Butler 1990; Martin 1991; Fox Keller 1992; McClintock 1995; Bryld and Lykke 2000; Franklin *et al.* 2000; Braidotti 2006). These researchers have used feminist critiques to investigate how science as a discourse and notions of the natural are used to support dominant ideologies.

In our final discussion, we ask what this enrolment says about social, rather than individual, aspects of ED, drawing inspiration from early medical sociology work on community responses to mental health (Eaton and Weil 1955) and recent qualitative studies of men's responses to ED (Oliffe 2005; 2006). By exploring alternative narratives of illness, we suggest, an alternative reading of erectile dysfunction and its subjects could be told.

Background

Science and technology studies use the term *enrolment* within ANT to denote how human and non-human agents are called on and woven into complicated networks (Latour 1993; 1998). Although it has been rightly criticized for implying a heroic, entrepreneurial actor in the process of enrolment (Star 1991), the concept is useful for our study because it articulates the sense that there are actors with specific interests (here, the pharmaceutical company Pfizer and its marketing experts) who use specific methods (those described in this chapter are discursive strategies) to involve heterogeneous constellations of human and non-human actors in the construction of a Swedish Viagra man. We will be using the concept of enrolment to examine how a specific web of actors – potential users, their medical doctors and their partners – is woven together by a discrete discourse to construct an identity and agenda for the Swedish Viagra man.

In Sweden, Viagra has been available by prescription since its approval in 1998, but, like the similar drugs Cialis and Levitra, it is not covered by the national subsidy programme for medicines. Thus, men can get a prescription for the drug, but they must pay for it out of their own pockets, which is unusual for the Swedish consumer. Produced and sold by the pharmaceutical company Pfizer, Viagra works physically in some men and in some situations by blocking the return of blood flowing out of the penis. Thus, if a man becomes aroused and blood flow to the penis increases, Viagra will help keep it there and produce an erection.

Discursively, however, Viagra does many other things. Viagra has, for example, changed our language about impotence in both English and Swedish. The marketing around Viagra has helped to introduce the term *erectile dysfunction* (ED) to the general public, replacing the more negative term *impotence* (Bordo 1998, 90; Potts 2004, 23). Masters and Johnson used the term *erectile dysfunction* in the

1950s (McLaren 2007, 221). In psychiatric discourse, erectile dysfunction has been articulated as a problem of arousal since the 1970s, when ED is defined as a problem of attaining and maintaining an erection sufficient for intercourse (APA 2000). Sexual response models within sex therapy have taken foremost physiology, but also behaviour (penetration) into account in defining healthy or non-healthy sex, which coloured the term *impotence* pejoratively, and later replaced it with the term *erectile dysfunction*. However, the medical community did not generally take up the term until it was adopted by urologists and popularized by Pfizer (see Bordo 1998; Marshall and Katz 2002; Loe 2004b; see Chapter 4 for the Swedish example). This rhetorical shift narrows the definition of what impotence is from a condition of the psyche, the emotions or the relationship, to a biomedical complaint (Marshall and Katz 2002; Tiefer 2006; McLaren 2007; Johnson 2008). Pfizer marketing has also introduced the concept of erectile quality (EQ) to expand the market to include younger men (Fishman and Mamo 2001, 181; Marshall 2002, 139), playing on 'erectile insecurity' (Tiefer 2006, 279). And, importantly, Viagra has been a phenomenon around which multiple, different, vested interests have gathered to sell it and construct the disease of ED, as Loe articulately shows in her examination of the US case (Loe 2004b).

As has been noted widely, Viagra has reinforced the definition of sex as penetration, and masculinity as the ability to achieve penetration, relying on a reworked version of the notion Sigmund Freud previously had reserved for the female mind: the 'anatomy is destiny' determinism of the naturalized body in the construction of the late modern male identity. The physicality of male embodiment boils down to the sexual (and not necessarily reproductive) performativity[4] of the visible sexual organ. Thus, within the Viagra discourse, as Baglia's (2005) study of Pfizer promotional material in the United States has shown, sexual performance is defined by a narrow sexual function model starting with arousal and progressing through erection, penetration and ejaculation. As long as a man can perform this penetrative sex, his masculinity is intact. The idea that penetration produces (or at least proves) masculinity reinforces the importance of penetration for both the sex act itself and the concept of sex-life expectancy. As sociologist Barbara Marshall notes, this concept of sex-life expectancy, with its calls to vigilant self-monitoring of healthy practices and appropriate sexual behaviour, relies on the disciplined individual taking responsibility for managing the risks of lost masculinity (i.e. lost ability to penetrate) even before 'old age' (Marshall 2006, 335). Viagra connects this individual responsibility to the medical and pharmaceutical networks within which Viagra is active, which also reinforces the scientism of sex and the naturalized body, attaching both to systems of expertise while simultaneously assigning responsibility for functionality to the man.

The Viagra discourse of sex relies on a three-step paradigm of arousal, penetration and ejaculation, and then demands Viagra as a solution to (age, stress or illness related) declining sexual performance (Plante 2006, 380). According to this discourse, a person (or couple) can maintain a successful sex life, as long as penetration is possible, that is with the help of Viagra. This idea ignores and tends to silence suggestions of alternative sexual practices and a sex life that is not dependent on penetration (Tiefer 2006). In this narrative, emotions all but disappear. And where they do play a role, responsibility for them is given to the partner, as we will discuss later.

Enrolling participants in the Viagra discourse

Examining the Swedish website it becomes apparent that Pfizer enrols three different groups of human participants to assist in constructing a subject position for men as potential consumers of Viagra: the men themselves; medical doctors; and the men's partners. Throughout the discourse, the Viagra pill is also enrolled as a non-human actor, nearly given a hero's identity.

Enrolling men

Men are enrolled through the information on the pages that constructs them as potential patients with ED. They are welcomed in what could be considered a respectful and tactful manner: 'Potency problems can be a sensitive issue in spite of the fact that many men – and their partners – are affected,'[5] they are told. The picture attached to the welcoming sentence, a photo of a tanned, grey-haired man in his fifties on his back with hands behind his head, smiling as he looks up into a blue sky that matches his blue t-shirt, suggests a relaxed, laid-back attitude. The blue colours of clothing and sky seem to allude to the iconic colour of Viagra and to Pfizer's logotype, and are a common feature of Viagra ads, as Loe (2004b) and Baglia (2005) have discussed. In the image and text, the cultural stigma of ED is mitigated by such a respectful yet relaxed approach. Further, the mode of address to the large number of men and their partners who suffer from ED normalizes the prevalence of the problem and works to alleviate the concern the visitor to this site may be experiencing. The accessibility of an easy, safe and comforting solution to erectile problems, in the form of the drug, is also highlighted by the film on the first page, complete with dancing, erect penises and reassuring statistics about how common ED is.

Aside from the overwhelming discourse of disease associated with erectile difficulties (including mention of cardiovascular disease, which will be discussed later), one of the primary tools used to enrol the men is an interactive quiz in which they are first asked to rate their sexual health (by answering a series of five questions) then encouraged to talk to their doctor. Unlike much of the other text on this site, the quiz is a short version of the International Index of Erectile Function (IIEF), and is directly translated from the US Viagra site.[6] As Marshall has discussed, this process of inviting quizzes, generous medical advice and sexual education effectively creates an ostensibly benevolent regime of self-surveillance on the website for the individual through assisted self-monitoring and remedial action (Marshall 2006, 356; see also Mamo and Fishman 2001; Baglia 2005). Such a mode of address, and ways of enticing and enrolling potential consumers of Viagra, can be read as part of a larger discourse, a sexual regimen of the individual. This sexual self-governance and monitoring, to borrow ideas from

Foucault, is centred on male penetration at the Viagra website. Given the flourishing market for self-health guides, books and websites and so forth, this mode of address is hardly surprising. This website merges the commercial aims of a product-selling site with sexual education and health advice in a manner characteristic of the rather recent new media genre of 'edutainment' where entertaining features such as quizzes and educational imagery blend for accessible, online display (Åsberg 2005).

Health matters are, in such genres, firmly placed within the world of consumerism, as detailed in Stacey's description of self-help literature in her cultural study of cancer (Stacey 1997). The Viagra consumer is enrolled into a mode of being sustained by the ideal of the self-caring subject position of a health consumer. In line with Stacey's work on health consumerism, this also resonates with what Rose and Novas termed 'biological citizenship' (Rose and Novas 2005, 14). The biological citizen invests heavily in self-education on health matters and develops the medical literacy needed to pursue a high-quality, self-sufficient, personally and socially 'responsible' lifestyle (Rose and Novas 2005, 14). Through the quiz on sexual health, the self-surveillance discourse redefines sexual health in a very specific, determinist way: sexual health for men is the achievement and maintenance of an erection and ability to complete intercourse. Their anatomy (particularly the functioning of certain parts of their anatomy) becomes their destiny.

The website not only encourages self-surveillance and individual responsibility, it also provides the tools for individuals to take on the task of monitoring and disciplining their erections:

> If you are being treated with potency medicine from Pfizer, you can receive support and encouragement for your treatment through the web.[7]
>
> Do you lack the time, desire or opportunity to pick up your medicine from the drugstore? Now you can have your impotence medicine delivered to your home by mail.
>
> Similarly, in a special section called the Potency Coach, illustrated by an animated cartoon figure with a megaphone, one finds that:
>
> The Potency Coach is an easy to use, interactive patient support that will help you achieve the expected and pre-determined results with your treatment. Here you can also find information about the underlying causes of potency problems and about other patients' experiences.

Working within a benevolent discursive frame to help him help himself, the website also reveals the assumption of a shy, Swedish man of few words implied by such a mode of address. The targeted subject is one who does not easily confide in his physician, especially not regarding sexually related matters, and must be reassured and coaxed to bring up the topic during a health care visit:

> Unfortunately, it is common that men hesitate before seeking help. This is a shame, since the vast majority of those who seek help can be successfully treated for their problems.

Perhaps surprisingly, it is not a sexually liberated or outspoken subject who is addressed, but someone rather inhibited when it comes to articulating sexual problems. From this arises a Swedish man who is non-articulate with respect to his own malleable body and sexual health, a man who might need encouragement when asking for a Viagra prescription at the doctor's office since doing so could be interpreted as a defeat in the masculinized struggle to control the body. Importantly, this can be read as a remarkable hands-on approach of Pfizer in facilitating the individual and his care of the self.

Enrolling doctors

Medical doctors are also enrolled through Pfizer's efforts on the Swedish www.potenslinjen.se website (beyond the infamous drug rep sales techniques [see Reidy 2005]). Part way down on the very first page, an anatomical sketch of a heart accompanies a text that reads 'Potency problems – an important warning sign' and delineates how potency problems might be the first 'useful' sign of cardiovascular diseases. It becomes clear that Viagra is not merely a matter of fleshy pleasures and an improved sex life, and that the ED Viagra is supposed to alleviate relates to serious health issues and even has a function as a first warning sign. Such medical appeals to cardiovascular health issues as linked to ED both play to the scientism of the naturalized body and work to medically legitimize Viagra. Swedish men seeking medical attention for ED are addressed as upstanding citizens taking responsibility for their personal overall health, and doctors are encouraged to help them with that. This use of medical complaints other than ED to legitimate Viagra can be read against the efforts in Sweden to associate Viagra with specific diseases rather than lifestyle choices as part of the debate over state subsidies (see Chapter 2).

The medical dimension of Viagra is further enhanced with a figure of authority that confirms both the relaxed personal tone and the urgency of the matter, namely a headshot of a physician in scrubs with a hint of a smile on the first page. The photo of the doctor creates a close proximity between medical authority and the potential Viagra consumer in another sense: the ambivalence of the picture in this setting suggests that even a medical doctor can have a use for Viagra. Most importantly, however, this small photo, emitting medical confidence and trustworthiness, serves a particular function within the website: to illustrate a search engine for finding a local, Viagra-friendly doctor. In addition to encouraging doctors to be 'proactive' in asking their patients about sexual function during routine exams and when taking medical histories,[8] Pfizer has included a national database of 'ED-aware' doctors, or 'affiliated experts' as Loe (2004b) calls them, which lets visitors to the website submit a query and generates a list of doctors near them who can be consulted for information about erectile dysfunction (and, presumably, for prescriptions of Viagra).

A clear example of local manifestations and adaptations of global marketing methods, the same type of database can be found on other national Viagra sites, also paired with suggested phrases that men can use when speaking to their doctors, addressing the fact that some men may find it difficult to bring up the subject of sexual dysfunction during an exam. On the Swedish site, men are told, 'When you meet your doctor, she or he will probably interview you and ask you questions about previous illnesses and if you are currently taking any medications. Try to provide as accurate information as possible, including if you still have early morning erections or if your erectile ability has disappeared suddenly or gradually. It may feel difficult to speak about these issues, but it is completely OK to be embarrassed. Remember that doctors are used to speaking about these things and their job is to help you.' In this way the men and doctors are also *positioned to enrol each other* and maintain each other's investment in the Viagra discourse. We suggest that this part of the Viagra website seems to connect biological citizenship with medical literacy and affiliated experts, to thus secure the commercial success of the drug.

Enrolling partners

On the Swedish site partners are also enrolled in the process of positioning men as subjects for whom Viagra is the solution to a waning sex life and/or issues of sexual dysfunction. Potency issues are continuously addressed as a joint problem, for the female partner as well as for the man. In a special section of the Swedish webpages, partners are told about the ways ED can affect a relationship, above all by letting coldness, distance and worry creep in and replace the sensitivity, nearness and trust that had been in the relationship before. On the connecting pages, partners are encouraged to be supportive, and then to let their partners know that treatments are available for the problem:

> Today there are many different treatment methods. There are medicines that are prescribed in connection with a doctor's visit. Apart from medical treatment, sometimes sexual therapy can be the most appropriate approach. It is good for you as a relative to know about this and to be able to support and encourage your partner to seek help.

The partners are also encouraged to order the free brochure 'A man's best support is by his side', published by Pfizer with a smiling, heterosexual couple on its front page. The way partners are enrolled to support the men experiencing ED plays strongly on the assumption that the partner is steadfastly (unreflectively?) consenting to reproduce certain practices and maintain a supportive position within a relationship with the man (cf. Potts *et al.* 2003). There is also information about how ED makes a man feel and what sorts of 'normal' behaviour it can provoke in one's partner. 'Many [men with ED] distance themselves from their partners simply to avoid conflict and to avoid situations which can lead to sex. Many develop a new hobby, immerse themselves in their work, or make sure they don't go to bed at the same time as their partner in the evening. Many consciously or subconsciously even create conflicts to avoid being close to their partner.' As this quote implies, sexual intercourse seems to be an active achievement, where 'success' needs to be granted. Moreover, the female partner has a supportive rather than a leading role in this sexual achievement which combines the traditional, passive recipient of penetration (waiting in the bed for her partner with the new hobby) with an active subject tasked with leading and directing the man to Viagra and/or sex therapy. She can guide him on his way, yet he is the doer behind the deed. This reverberates with the traditional assumption about heterosexual femininity as sexual passivity and masculinity as sexual activity, but more importantly it also points to the enormous effort by the woman that in reality lies behind achieving the 'passivity', which can confirm his active and valuable status as a heterosexual male. There are many subtle manoeuvres, enticing practices and persuasive, yet necessarily non-direct rhetorical moves a woman must master in order to achieve the right amount of sex-inspiring passivity. A lot of hard work lies behind her 'passive' affirmation of his masculinity.

A specific section of the Swedish website is dedicated to the prescriptive discursive patterns available to the partner. As the main heading on the partners' page suggests, she should ask herself how 'can I help?' to receive the answer, 'Speak to and encourage: It is best to speak openly with your partner; support each other'.

In this section of the Swedish webpage one finds a discussion about how ED and the normal behaviour it provokes in men can make the partner feel. These partner responses build on feelings of guilt and inadequacy. However, the partners are encouraged to persevere and help their men seek help because 'When one has received help and solved the problem, many discover that their relationship has in fact become stronger.' Again, the partner's discursive work is one of maintaining a seemingly effortless and natural attitude that avoids putting pressure on her partner and is achieved by another rhetorical strategy here provided by the Viagra site text, namely the 'we'. She can address her sexual needs and his sexual problems if they are addressed as a 'we' issue, enrolling a sexual dyad, a figure of heterosexual complementarity.

Within the Swedish context, it is worth noting that pre-Viagra (prior to 1998) medical advice about impotence underlined how important it was for doctors to warn their patients that merely solving a man's inability to produce an erection would not necessarily solve relationship problems (Olsson *et al.* 1995), something the Pfizer information seems to belie. Internationally, this assertion can be read in light of a Japanese study where a survey on the level of satisfaction derived from using Viagra indicated that while the male patient was extremely satisfied, his partner was not satisfied at all. Women reported their husbands' erections as troublesome, that they had to use supplements to increase vaginal lubrication and in some cases even take hormones (Castro-Vázquez 2006, 123). Loe (2004a) and Potts and colleagues (2003) also provide examples of women's responses to and concerns about Viagra use in the United States, demonstrating a wide diversity in opinions and practices. Additional studies on Swedish women's accounts of Viagra would here be needed, but looking at the website it is clear that the female partner, since heterosexuality becomes further implied in the illustrative photos of both older and younger heterosexual couples that frame the text, is enrolled as responsible for the man's health and for their relationship; she can help him help himself to become the

Viagra-empowered, potent man. At the website, her task becomes one of ensuring that penetrative intercourse can occur, since sexual intercourse is what consolidates the relationship and makes it strong. Through the figure of the sympathetic partner conjured up on the website, the responsibility not only for the general health and well-being of the man but also for the emotional health of the couple is presented as a feminized task.

It is here, in the partner section, that emotions and feelings are mentioned on the website with the references to coldness, distance, worry, sensitivity, nearness, trust, guilt and encouragement. Physiologically, Viagra only works if a man is sexually aroused in the first place, so partners are encouraged to help achieve Viagra's success by ensuring the necessary feelings are in place. Thus responsibility for the emotional aspects of sex, not just the relationship, is also effectively given to the partner. Partners are reminded that ED is 'the man's symptom, the couple's shared problem', so the partner is directed to 'speak to and encourage' the man. She is the one who in practice can confirm his potency. Her assignment within the Viagra discourse is to manage this talk as she takes the emotional responsibility for discussing and reflecting over the role of sex for their relationship. Here, too, emotions come into the discourse but so do the co-constitutive agencies of medical expertise, female partners and Viagra as embodied, chemical effect as well as an expectation on virile manhood giving shape to the ideal Viagra man. Partners are encouraged to learn about ED because, 'with knowledge in hand, you will find it easier to speak with your partner. Together you can discuss your feelings and thoughts, and give each other support, and in the end, solve your relationship problems'.

We suggest that this assignment of emotions and responsibility for the relationship's well-being to the female partner enables her to legitimately address the problem of ED as a shared issue. Within the discourse on the Viagra pages, the tool she is often given to solve the problem is the little blue pill, but because of the particularly Swedish, legally dictated, 'informational' role of the website, the partner is also provided with information about alternative treatments like sexual therapy (even if this information is sparse and even as the site is branded in a very Viagra blue). But as we will discuss later, enrolling the partner in the ED discourse this way could also open alternative solutions and alternative definitions of the problem.

Discussion

In our analysis, we have identified three enrolled participants the website addresses to help create a subject position for the consuming Viagra man. The first of these is the male patient, for whom anatomy and age become his destiny, but who can consume Viagra to control that destiny and discipline it in line with youthful expectations. The second is the doctor, both enrolled to help ensure the male patient can access Viagra and used to represent scientism, which legitimates the use of Viagra by associating it with networks of scientific expertise. And thirdly, the partner of the patient is also enrolled in the process of creating a subject position for the

Viagra-consuming man. Responsibility for his emotions is given to his partner, who simultaneously consents to supporting a pharmaceutical solution for the man and the relationship.

The enrolment of these three participants in the commercial discourse creates a network of actors who can perform the desire for, distribution of and context to contribute to successful use of a pharmaceutical as a solution to impotence. Their presence in the commercial Viagra discourse is particularly striking when one considers that they all but disappeared from the medical discourse around Viagra when it was introduced in 1998. As Chapter 4 discusses, the Swedish medical journal *Läkartidningen* supported a very heterogeneous definition of impotence and impotent patients in the early 1990s, one which recognized many different types of men with different reasons behind their impotence, and which encouraged the involvement of partners during treatment, enrolling the partner in much the same way as the Viagra website does (Olsson *et al.* 1995, 313). This approach was not necessarily benign; the imagined partner was a woman in this (also) very heterosexual discourse, and she was ascribed a narrow position in the discourse: 'Men and women have different ways of expressing themselves and therefore misunderstandings can easily arise. Women must learn to be clearer and men to be more receptive' (Olsson *et al.* 1995, 313). Her ideal sexuality was also limited: unthreatening, dependent on and receptive to her male partner's desires. 'The best help for a man with disappointing erections is, besides his own courage to speak about it, an understanding and sensual partner who is sexually keen but not demanding' (Olsson *et al.* 1995, 314). However, with the 1998 advent of Viagra, the medical discourse in *Läkartidningen* narrowed the definition of an impotent patient to the male penis and removed the varied social and sexual backgrounds, and actors, which had previously been present. Yet, in the commercial discourse, the partner and factors like stress and tiredness are present alongside Viagra.

Despite the stigma attached to impotence and the common assumption that men would not want to talk about ED (as the nudging encouragement provided by www.potenslinjen.se implies), qualitative research (primarily interview studies) on men who are dealing with erectile dysfunction shows that not all men deal with their ED problems alone and in silence. Many men are already enrolling medical professionals and partners in their quest for a solution (Oliffe 2005; 2006; Grace *et al.* 2006). These men turn to medical professionals to procure treatments for their impotence (Viagra and similar drugs, but also injections and vacuum pump treatments) and some men engage their partners both in treatment therapies and as discussion partners with whom they can talk about their difficulties and explore alternative sexual practices (Oliffe 2005). As much current research within masculinities studies supports, men's experience of illness, especially a condition as related to masculinity as erectile dysfunction, is influenced by how the men and those around them, that is the network of actors enrolled in definition and solution work, think about and practise masculinity (cf. Marshall and Katz 2002; Aucoin and Wessersug 2006; Sandberg 2011). These studies also suggest that some men who experience sexual dysfunction are already comfortable using a network of actors to help them both define their problem and seek treatment options.

We ask, then, how this practice and these enrolled actors (patients, doctors and partners) differ from the enrolment we have observed on the Swedish webpage. The obvious answer, of course, is that in the conversations detailed in Oliffe (2005) the partner pair can explore non-pharmaceutical solutions. But we would like to suggest that the type of 'enrolment' that the men are displaying is also different in another way. Their enrolment is an activity which creates a community of people, all of whom can help to define the medical problem as medical *or not* and as a problem *or not*. And, importantly, it is also a community that seems to at least tacitly recognize that the solution, when there is one, is one that needs to be acted on and participated in by more than just the man. In particular, these interview studies would seem to highlight the partner's need to be active in defining the problem, and also the solution, as co-produced and as something that both parts of the couple are actively participating in. This is in contrast to perceiving ED as a disease of the penis and the penis alone, and for which responsibility to enact a solution (take a pill which will maintain an erection) is the man's. As we have shown, in the Viagra discourse, the partner is enrolled to help the man see how important it is for him to take Viagra. This demands a significant amount of work on her part, actively enabling the man to recognize the problem as ED and the solution as Viagra. An alternative would be for partners to be enrolled as participants who can also define alternative sexual practices and solutions.

Thinking about the enrolment of not only new, male patients, but also their doctors and their partners, we were reminded of an early study of mental health by Eaton and Weil (1955), which found that relatively isolated, Anabaptist communities' responses to patients who developed mental illness were very different than the response to mental illness found in the wider American society at the time. Rather than isolating the individual, institutionalizing him or her, and stigmatizing the patient, the Hutterite communities tried to help the individual continue to play a role in the community, contributing and working as best they could, and being cared for by their family during the course of the illness (Eaton and Weil 1955, 212). Reading this study today, it is obvious that it was written before the pharmaceutical industry had colonized the discourse of mental illness, and illness in general. Rather than talking about patient-centred, individualized cures to illness, the study relied on concepts of social cohesion, social structures and group expectations as explanatory models and as treatment options. It pays special attention to sociological variables, the cultural and social dimensions of health (Eaton and Weil 1955, 25).

We are not suggesting that a theory of social cohesion and mental health from 1955 may be a good way to reinterpret erectile dysfunction. But as a reminder that our research material, our observations and our interpretations are influenced by the paradigm within which we are working, it is very useful. Going back to the material we have discussed in this chapter, and looking at the way patients, doctors, partners and pills are enrolled in the production of Viagra consumers, we see first that these actors are enrolled to produce pharmaceutical consumption as a treatment option. Secondly, the men and their partners are not discussed as explanatory factors. Although it may seem unnecessary to reintroduce the partner as the source of impotence (for a discussion of historical, cultural and social explanations of impotence, see McLaren (2007)), this enrolment can explain what other critical research on Viagra has shown; that its existence and doctors' participation in its prescription practices have created ED. Social structures (the pharmaceuticalized framework) and group expectations (of lifelong sexual activity and successful ageing) have contributed to the 'epidemic' of erectile dysfunction. The illness, itself, is constructed by the enrolled actors. Only then can they be engaged as a network to (help the man) find a solution. Starting from this insight, we ask: how might these same human actors be enrolled into creating a different solution? If Viagra was not available, what solutions could this cast of characters work together to find? Who/what else could possibly be enrolled? And how would the concept of ED change?

Like mental illness, impotence has traditionally been a situation that is not generally flouted or discussed publicly. Therefore we find it interesting that the Viagra solution suddenly enrols a wider group of actors to help the man find a solution. The Viagra solution demands these other actors; the regulatory framework in Sweden means that doctors are a gatekeeper to the drug; and Viagra's reliance on sexual desire means that the sexual partner can be important to initiate, develop or maintain arousal. What we are asking is: if these three groups of actors (men, their doctors and their partners) can be enrolled to address ED through Viagra, how could they be enrolled to address ED without Viagra? How would a distributed response to ED place responsibility for dealing with the problem at the relationship(s) and community level rather than only by individual?

We suggest that these examples, both Oliffe's qualitative research on men with impotence (Oliffe 2005; 2006) and the pre-Viagra treatment advice for doctors, show that enrolling a wider community to respond to a health issue is possible. Enrolling a larger network of actors can involve finding and supporting alternative behaviours, alternative demands and alternative expectations, both by and of the 'individual' with a condition, such as erectile dysfunction, and by the people around him who are also affected by it.

Notes

1 An earlier version of this chapter has been published as Johnson, E. and Åsberg, C. (2012). Enrolling the Swedish Viagra Man. *Science and Technology Studies*, *25* (2), 46–60.

2 Accessed in October 2007, February and April 2008, November 2009 and October 2015.

3 This is in contrast to another Pfizer-sponsored website, www.viagra.se, which is framed as an informational site for medical professionals. The different readership is constructed to legally avoid DTC advertising of Viagra.

4 We would like to point out that this performativity is more directly connected to specific physical actions than the discursive performativity often found in gender studies, that is Butler's (1990) work.

5 www.potenslinjen.se, accessed 4 November 2009.

6 www.viagra.com

7 The quotes cited later are (unless otherwise mentioned) taken from www.potenslinjen.se, accessed 5 November 2009.

8 This encouragement and advice in how to meet and speak with patients with ED is presented on the website http://viagra.se, which is directed solely to health professionals (Accessed 28 October 2007).

7 Viagra selfhood

Pharmaceutical advertising and the visual formations of Swedish masculinity[1]

Cecilia Åsberg and Ericka Johnson

In this chapter, we will investigate the visual configuration of what we term a *Swedish Viagra imaginary*, a cultural phantasy landscape that produces and reproduces certain subject positions of great interest for feminists and other scholars invested in social change. More precisely, we interrogate a set of key images presented by the Pfizer-sponsored website for potential Swedish Viagra customers with erectile dysfunction in order to explore how this particular Viagra imaginary provides reference points for shared and collective identities. We explore here the visual formation, and the naturalization, of the nationally shaped masculinity of the potential consumers of Viagra at a Swedish-language site, www.potenslinjen.se/,[2] the same site discussed in Chapter 6. This site is produced by the pharmaceutical company Pfizer for the explicit purpose of providing the Swedish public with health information on erectile problems.

Drawing on feminist science studies, cultural studies and medical technology studies, we argue that Viagra is a cultural phenomenon, or rather a material-semiotic node for discursive production and identity formation – one inflected by individualized health concerns as well as by the social authority of medicine and the compelling appeal of so-called lifestyle pharmaceuticals. Following masculinity theorist and feminist cultural scholar Graham Dawson, a cultural imaginary, as a kind of cultural phantasy landscape, is not monolithic and not hegemonic, but fluid and multiple. It consists of 'those vast networks of interlinking discursive themes, images, motifs, and narrative forms that are publicly available within a culture at any one time, and articulate its psychic and social dimensions' (Dawson 1994, 48). Cultural communities not only mirror but also continually reinvent themselves through cultural imaginaries, as these are sites of identity negotiation and formation.

The reality-producing and identity-constituting effect of such discursive activities is why it is of the essence to study emerging subjectivities, such as those appearing publicly at Viagra websites. Moreover, in line with other critical studies of pharmaceutical use and promotion,[3] we argue that Viagra is a feminist issue. The tendency to divide the psychic, the social and the techno-scientific into separate domains of knowledge has been resisted in a rich body of work, including that of feminist cultural studies of techno-science, and is an interdisciplinary mode in which we feel largely at home; see Åsberg and Johnson (2009) and Johnson (2008). We attempt to align and establish cross-disciplinary dialogue between cultural theory and gender studies, media ethnography and studies of science, medicine and technology in society. Our work implies that we see sexual difference within a cultural theory setting, understood as the effect of the human subject's entry into the symbolic systems of its culture. While subjectivity is neither universal nor ahistorical, it is the product of structuring social relations, shaped by materialities and physical embodiment as much as by social phantasy. Shared and collective, these phantasies organize a screen through which the material world appears and social relations are experienced. As cultural imaginaries, they furnish public forms, organize knowledge of the social world and give shape to phantasies that are constitutive of, in this case, masculine identities. Our method is materialist in that it tries to stay clear of both cultural and biological determinisms while approaching material-semiotic phenomena discursively (cf. Haraway 1989). The target of our study here is not the lived, sensuous body-self, but the hermeneutic, cultural embodiment of Viagra masculinity in discourse.

Our analysis builds on discussions of the promotion of Viagra (a drug marketed by Pfizer since 1998 for men and couples as a cure for erectile dysfunction) and the construction of masculinities and sexuality as a lifelong duty and health concern of the individual also in other comparative national contexts, such as the United States, New Zealand and Japan (see Bordo 1998; Fishman and Mamo 2001; Marshall 2002; Potts 2004; Marshall 2006; Tiefer 2006; Johnson 2008). Like other critical readings of Viagra (Fishman and Mamo 2001; Marshall 2006; Tiefer 2006; Vares and Braun 2006), we are examining the construction of *ideal users* of Viagra and especially the nationalized, classed, racialized and sexualized identities they are assigned. This, however, does not imply that we naively aim to reveal any kind of Viagra ideology as a singular site of reality distortion produced by the discursive operations of Big Pharma (ideology critique). The political driving forces of social change are today much more complex and highly individualized, which makes us interested in the creation of cultural appeal rather than the creation of (hegemonic) consent. In order to investigate in local detail, for instance, how retiring sexually became a sign of pathology through the new Viagra discourse, we are aligning slightly different insights from feminist approaches to intersectionality[4] (identity as a crossroad of intersecting social categories such as gender, age, ethnicity and embodiment) with the notions of the social imaginary and subject positioning (the cultural encouragement for one to take up a specific sense of self) from visual cultural studies, and further, with previous work within medical sociology and feminist science studies on the ideological processes of medicalization and naturalization.

Interrogating the many cultural dimensions of 'the natural' as a rhetorical device at work in the Viagra imaginary, we consult the work that a range of feminist scholars working on (or in) science, medicine and technology have produced since the late 1970s on the powerful, ideological processes of *naturalization* (cf. Merchant 1980; Haraway 1989; Butler 1990; Fox Keller 1992; McClintock

1995; Bryld and Lykke 2000; Franklin *et al.* 2000). It has, through such research, become clear that authoritative speech of the natural has maintained stereotypical definitions of sex and gender throughout late modernity.

In the case we present, Viagra seems – somewhat oxymoronically – to be naturalizing a hegemonic form of masculinity as closely associated with virility, and as determined by erectile capacity for penile penetration of the female body. On one hand, such masculine subjectivity is about successful ageing and the maintaining of an autonomous and androcentric, well-defined and impenetrable selfhood, one disassociated from health problems and embodiment in general. On the other hand, Viagra discourse invites interrogations of *volatile* masculinity and male ageing, pharmaceutical incorporation and prosthetic virility, and of commerce in liaison with medical science. These paradoxical Viagra connections function in direct opposition to the teleological ethos of science imagined to rationally and purposefully promote social development. This is evidenced by the narrative of how Viagra, with the active substance sildenafil citrate, came into commercial existence as the accidental result of heart medicine trials in which the male test subjects reported regained capacities for erectile functioning, and is an example of how we see Viagra performing ontologically as a curious material-semiotic node, an entangled case of meaning and materiality with some unexpected outcomes, especially regarding the choreography of selfhood, which we see as inflected by the formative powers of gender, nationality and sexuality.

Delineating the glocal of the creation of new techno-social identities around drugs, we discuss what we see as the performance of 'Swedish' elements of the Viagra man constructed through the text and images on the site, as this collective identity is imagined as slightly different from that presented in the advertisements that have helped to market Viagra to the US and New Zealand customer base (see www.viagra.com and www.viagra.co.nz). US advertising has seen a conceptual shift from impotence to erectile dysfunction (ED), and later to erectile quality (EQ) – as a much more inclusive category of erectile insecurity. These shifts, closely associated to the use of Viagra to maintain masculinity against the threats of ageing and other stresses in life, have meant that the potential market for the drug has expanded from older men with serious medical problems (as represented by early Bob Dole endorsements) to ageing but active, sporty types (presented through endorsements by football stars like Pele and baseball stars in the United States), to 'every man' as in the ads with non-famous, regular Joes (called 'Svenssons' in Swedish) in their thirties. Much of the critical research about Viagra has so far come from the United States and New Zealand, two countries which allow DTC advertising of prescription medicine (see Mamo and Fishman 2001; Elliott 2003; Loe 2004a; Moynihan and Cassels 2005). DTC advertising of pharmaceuticals creates a media climate that allows drug companies like Pfizer to deliver information about their products to the general population through billboards, television, infomercials, magazines, newspapers, radio and so forth, pumping out a Viagra message and producing a Viagra-primed, ED-aware audience (Potts and Tiefer 2006, 268). The messages about Viagra are also mirrored in jokes, television programmes and movies, documentaries and news reports, reflecting the fact that the line between paid advertising and media coverage is often blurry. This has bearing on our case study as well. Medical and popular imagery (with an almost global scope) take part in co-shaping a Viagra imaginary that provides a backdrop onto which virility can be measured and masculine subjectivities positioned. As discussed in Chapter 6, because of the ban on DTC advertising of prescription medicine, the Swedish situation is slightly different (although this ban is not always easy to enforce). (Pfizer ran an ad campaign for Viagra on bus-stop billboards in 2004, and satellite television broadcasts from abroad have created a loophole for television ads as well; see Zetterqvist *et al.* (2015).) As mentioned earlier, Viagra has also figured largely in the collective psyche in Sweden as a subject both of newspaper articles and of debate, thanks in large part to the drawn-out discussions and court cases about whether the Swedish health care system would subsidize Viagra.

Concerned with the co-constitutive work of national and global imagination (Anderson 1983), and with what has been theorized as the unfinished and open-ended 'new universalisms of global culture' (Stacey 2000), we study how digital imagery employed within pharmaceutical marketing positions embodied subjects through appeals to both the national and the natural. Appeals to the national and the natural are highly potent cultural tropes through which identity formation can take place (Williams 1980; Franklin *et al.* 2000). National differences, understood in line with Benedict Anderson's (1983) anthropological notion of nationhood as non-essential imagined communities, are here comparative indicators of the glocal dimensions of the Viagra imaginary. While Anderson assumed that national media, like everyday print press or museums, maintained such a collective imaginary, we propose to investigate how such national imagery today also is co-constituted by commercial, sometimes conflicting, global flows of imagery in general, and by the pharmaceutical industry on the Internet in particular. It is in that vein we closely read the cultural processes that produce the subject position of a specific type of Swedish man as a potential consumer of Viagra. This ideal consumer, as he is addressed in the web text and imagined in the selected photos, is a cultural figuration we refer to as the Swedish Viagra man.

Naturalizing the Swedish Viagra man

An example of how Pfizer's Swedish erectile dysfunction site for the general public takes an active part in the public negotiation of the meaning of masculinity as related to penetrative sex is a list published on the site of the top ten characteristics of 'a manly man'. This list is based on a public poll and can be read against the backdrop of a rather large interest in issues of gender, in what constitutes 'manliness' and 'womanliness', in Swedish public debate. Gender is a positive notion in Sweden, yet the content of such national awareness, informed as it is by decades of gender equality policy work, sometimes amounts to no more than an uncritical celebration of bipolar difference (Elvin-Nowak and Thomsson 2001, 409). However, in the summer of 2003, Pfizer hired a nationally renowned polling company to create a top ten list of what Swedish people associated with manliness, and the result reads as follows:[5]

1. To be practical and handy (a handyman of sorts)
2. To have good potency (presumed sexual)
3. To have a well-paying job
4. To have an attractive partner
5. To have a physically fit, muscular body
6. To have an attractive outer appearance
7. To be interested in sports
8. To be always ready for sex
9. To own technical gadgets
10. To have a cool car

The desire to perform an all-around able-bodied, and even enhanced (with cars, gadgets or other status-raising attributes) form of masculinity is clearly a defining feature of the potential Viagra consumer. As an underlying and unarticulated assumption, such a notion is, in a commercial, yet serious health informational setting like this website, spoken of in terms of 'good potency' and visualized through imagery of active men appearing in non-erotic, everyday life settings as to not risk 'indecent', or even homoerotic, associations. This might be regarded as somewhat surprisingly prudish in a national setting famous for its high level of sexual education. Viagra has, however, been promoted in accordance with a class-related sense of 'respectability', and such a legitimating mode of address is achieved at this site through the staging of health information and references to medical professionals.

Next to the list, the visitor is given the opportunity to vote online for which of the top four points s/he finds most manly. The results from that direct online poll name, unsurprisingly, potency as the number one characteristic and handiness as number two. This poll also indicates how Viagra, while in a limited and framed manner on this site, actually is very effective in inviting the addressed web visitor to contemplate the meaning of masculinity as strongly linked to, or even framed by, erectile capacity. Possible anxieties around potency are also in such a benevolent manner (as an open poll) simultaneously alleviated (in how it becomes a collective issue) and enforced (by the underlining of potency as the most important manly feature). The solution to any private feelings of inadequacy is placed in the hands of the individual, as he (or a female partner) on the website is encouraged to ask a medical professional for a Viagra prescription. This echoes the recurring signature of US television commercials for pharmaceutical products where the viewer, at the end of the ad, is always prompted to ask his or her physician about the new drug. We read this as part of a larger transnational discourse of 'biological citizenship' (Rose and Novas 2005), where the multinational company is positioned as a benevolent assistant to the good and healthy sex life that, in the website rhetoric, becomes the duty of the individual consumer.

This able-bodied and individualized ideal masculinity, as it emerges in the list, is to a large part construed in antagonist relation to common associations to lived femininity (soft embodiment, a low-paid job, dependency, not always ready for sex and less interested in male sports, cars and technical gadgets). In turn, this points to a phantasy masculinity inflected by class, sexual orientation and age, as some of the gendered ideals (owning a cool car) seem formatted already within teenage boyhood, although usually only attainable in adult life. Of note is that this list is framed and presented at the blue-tinted Viagra website along with a picture of a man in a Viagra-blue overall changing a tyre. By analogue, Viagra seems an easy solution, as a technical quick fix, to any kind of common feelings of insufficient manhood related to being able-bodied overall. The image of the man changing the tyre manages to displace a commonplace cultural fetish of ability where almost everything mundane and less than erotic (like changing tyres) that defines such masculinity seems hinged on erectile capacities. While clean in design, the website imagery is perhaps not completely devoid of any hints or visual reference to intercourse as a forceful male accomplishment, as the man is prosthetically enhanced by his phallic jack and tyre iron, screwing wheel lugs on an equally Viagra-blue car.

Many of the other images on the site, however, portray romantic couples. The Swedish Viagra man seems to predominately appear, whether alone and able-bodied or in a relationship, through the discourses of heteronormativity (Butler 1990). Nonetheless, there is an ambiguity to the imagery that opens up for slightly different interpretations. We found one photo on the Swedish website where a couple's sunlit feet are flirtatiously entangled on a bed with white bed sheets, where the gender of the couple is hard to decipher. It could be the feet of two men, or even two women, just as well as the feet of a heterosexual couple. As an example of erectile desires not being confined to heterosexual men, this picture could in fact lend itself to the possibility of portraying a male homosexual couple. Aligning the erectile function of the drug with sensuous imagery of couples or active men sustains, however, a reductive idea where penetration becomes the sole means through which relationships can be confirmed and a sexual act manifested. Also, it becomes clear that Viagra is not intended as a drug for the single man wishing to enjoy masturbatory sex on his own.

The masculine identity on the Swedish website is marked with nationalized signifiers of socioeconomic class in several ways. For example, on one of the information pages about facts and myths of impotence, there is the myth that 'wet dreams give early morning erections'. Nocturnal erections are then explained by the assertion that 'When a man is sleeping his penis exercises to keep in shape. A healthy man will have an erection approximately every 70th to 100th minute when he is sleeping, regardless of whether he is thinking about sex or tax deductibles.' This same message appears in the short film on the website's first page. The reference to tax deductibles, in a country of progressive income taxes and, until recently, high capital gains taxes, could be interpreted as an appeal to the interests of the middle and upper-middle classes, or, at least, to the desire to be associated with financially savvy methods of avoiding taxes. Thus, it becomes part of respectable upper-middle-class life to consume Viagra.

Perhaps most clearly indicative of Swedishness and its association with healthy, physical activity in the outdoors is the dominant imagery of people (men and couples) in wilderness settings. As a collective phantasy of national belonging and camaraderie, the overall use of this imagery can be seen in many commercials for a wide range of products in Sweden. We feel that one image on the site in particular poignantly plays on a charged version of Swedish nature. This image has a blurred, male body jumping into the water in what appears to be a summer day in the Swedish archipelago. It draws on a widely viewed beer commercial from the 1990s. This commercial, with a distinguishable aesthetic reproduced in several versions over the past decades, has come to represent the much-sought-after, idealized Swedish summer. It is a commercial for Pripp's Blue Beer which shows mixed-sex groups of white Swedes in their late twenties and early thirties gathering on the cliffs of the Swedish coast on what is obviously a crisp, yet warm and salty afternoon during the summer holidays. This group of Swedes, with their well-built, muscular bodies and attractive and slender partners, all wearing swimwear and seemingly without make-up, brings with them a large case of Pripp's Blue Beer and spends the duration of the commercial barbequing, sailing or jumping in and out of the water while laughing to the background sounds of a then-popular Swedish pop-song, 'Blue, blue winds and water'.[6] After more than a decade, this advertisement was still running on Swedish television, and the imagery from the commercial has fastened in the cultural imaginary of what constitutes Swedishness; namely, naturalness and freedom merged with an aestheticized form of summer night melancholia. Serendipitously for Viagra, 'Blue' is the iconic brand name of a particular Pripp's beer and, for millions of Swedes tuned into popular culture, it represents blue water, blue skies and a laid-back, yet youthful attitude of sexual yearning (blue as in nostalgic, yet not unhappy, feelings) – all staged within a coastal setting very much like that in an image on the Viagra website.

The www.potenslinjen.se site taps into this Swedish imagery of the outdoor life, where several other pictures feature men and couples by the seaside. A rather simple yet highly effective aesthetic works thus to naturalize Swedish masculinity and connect it to Viagra. We would like to emphasize the central role of scenic landscapes and visualized Swedish nature as the photographic backdrop in this process of naturalizing the Swedish Viagra man. At the same time, class plays in the background. Access to the seaside, to a private sailboat that enables access to unpopulated islands, cliffs and bathing areas during the short summer, is a privilege that is somewhat restricted to members of the capital-owning classes. Such an upper- and middle-class summer lifestyle is thus the iconic ideal and unique selling point for both this rather widely accessible beer and the slightly less accessible pharmaceutical. It is a national phantasy of Swedish nature and the yearning nature of Swedes as they long for that 'blue' summer feeling. We contend that the Viagra illustrations on www.potenslinjen.se effectively make use of such a blue and youthfully sexual, class-coded and nature-loving, national imaginary of white Swedish masculinity.

This nationalized construction of a middle-class Viagra man in Sweden should be seen in light of the prolonged court deliberations over subsidizing Viagra for the general public, which was finally decided in March 2008. As Viagra is not subsidized in Sweden (see Chapter 2), individuals have to cover the full cost of prescriptions. In a country in which all people are covered by state health care which substantially subsidizes most pharmaceutical products, the idea of paying for a drug, particularly a lifestyle drug, is relatively foreign. Many people would probably think twice before purchasing Viagra with their own money when they are accustomed to receiving medication much cheaper. Thus, the fact that Viagra is not subsidized means that the market for the drug is probably smaller than it would otherwise be, at least for Viagra received through a doctor's prescription, which is the method of procurement www.potenslinjen.se promotes. The film on the first webpage claims that 100,000 Swedes purchase Viagra illegally over the Internet and warns strongly against this. Pfizer has probably therefore consciously chosen to market the drug to those social groups with more expendable income.

The image construction of Viagra on the site is also involved in positioning men as sufferers of legitimate potency problems related to underlying health concerns, thus avoiding connotations to Viagra as a recreational sex drug for party-happy youngsters. The target group is instead respectable yet mundane, middle-aged, Swedish, middle-class men, perhaps residing in the northern countryside. The images on www.potenslinjen.se all depict a very traditional and a very white Scandinavian man. This despite the fact that Sweden is, today, a multi-ethnic country with a significant urban population.

Among the photos illustrating the claims about potency, health and Viagra, there are, besides the medical expert (a white, slightly balding, middle-aged yet vital-looking man in glasses and blue scrubs), relatively few portraits of men. One exception to this is an image which shows the face of the naturalized, Swedish Viagra man in a winter coat in front of an unpopulated and cold, coastal landscape. Most photographed people are otherwise depicted with their backs to the camera from afar so their faces cannot be discerned, or metonymically represented through parts of their (tanned, yet white-skinned) bodies, like the entangled feet belonging to the couple in bed. Conversely, the somewhat older man in a winter coat looks confidently back at the audience with cheeks blushed by the cold. The untamed shoreline in a frosty landscape associates him (and Viagra) to the wilderness rather than a cosmopolitan life. It links directly to notions of nature and the natural.

Ideas of the natural are often working through a cultural imperative of preservation, of safeguarding the natural as if God-given, and it is probably the most powerful trope through which subject positioning and identity formation works (Williams 1980; Franklin *et al.* 2000). The drug Viagra can be conceptualized as natural, as it is presented in Pfizer marketing material, since it enables men an assumed 'normal' control over their bodily functions. *It makes naturalized masculinity possible*. Taking the pill merely enables 'nature to take its course' (Mamo and Fishman 2001, 20). So at the Pfizer website, the task of the biomedical drug industry seems, somewhat oxymoronically, to be one of 'seconding nature'

(Franklin *et al.* 2000, 21f). In other words, it is one of preserving naturalized masculinity through the prosthetic virility Viagra can provide.

The imagery online conceptualizes both Swedish nature and Viagra as a drug seconding such nature, as a quality of both the inner, personal and outer, physical landscapes of the people depicted. From landscapes by the sea in the southern coastal areas or winters up north, images of Swedish nature sustain notions of Viagra as a normal and natural ingredient through the idea of 'letting nature take its course'. The Swedish man becomes one with the enhanced natural surroundings, as Viagra becomes one with the 'natural' Swedish man. It is with surprising ease that the marketing of a pharmacological product can associate ageing Northern manhood to harsh and untamed landscapes, as it seems sustained by gendered national demographics where women move south to work in the urban areas and men stay in the north for the fishing and hunting. Such a phantasy of seconded nature remains by implication unsubdued by civilization (gender equality discourse or multiculturalism) as it takes on the oppositional characteristic of feminized and multicultural cosmopolitanism. Interestingly, Swedish masculinity works here not in opposition to nature and wildlife, but through Viagra, as realigned with natural virility. It seems almost as if the defeminization of the north requires the enforcement of heterosexual masculinity. Viagra virility, also as the commodification of men's sexual health, presents itself as a striking and counterintuitive account of white masculinity coupled with a national phantasy of uncompromised, and uncompromising, nature.

Concluding remarks

In this investigation of the Viagra imaginary and the techno-social identities it enacts, we dealt predominately with identity-forming intersections such as a nationalized (Swedish), middle-class sexuality and naturalized, white masculinity. This is a masculinity which nonetheless is conspicuously malleable, vulnerable and a target for a virility-enhancing drug like Viagra. Importantly, we dealt with a visual and spectacular kind of embodied subjectivation to both public and medical scrutiny, a subjectivity creating processes otherwise historically preserved for the female body (Jordanova 1989; McClintock 1995). In fact, Pfizer has positioned the drug as important to 'every' man through discourses that present masculinity as the opposite of sexual impotence. Masculinity is equated with 'successful' sex, a very specific, narrowly defined act of penetration in (usually heterosexual) intercourse. Being able to perform with an erect penis in this specific way is equated with manhood. By aligning masculinity with physiological sexual performance and promising reliable performance with the assistance of a pill, this discourse asserts that a man can maintain his masculinity regardless of age. Inflected by a strong sense of constant vigilance or disciplining of the male body, Viagra discourse demands individual responsibility so to manage the risk of losing such a virile masculinity even before one enters 'old age' (Marshall 2006, 355). As the consumption of Viagra promises a youthful sexuality long into 'old age', it also becomes another building block in the construction of an ideology about 'successful ageing' as the responsibility of the individual as s/he is framed within a liberal discourse of individualized self-care and biological citizenship (cf. Stacey 1997, 2000; Rose and Novas 2005; Åsberg and Johnson 2009).

Our observations about the glocal images of the Swedish Viagra man can be read in line with previous research, which has already shown that Pfizer adjusts its marketing strategy to appeal to local consumers. For example, whereas in the US advertisements for Viagra have used baseball stars to promote Viagra, in New Zealand, Pfizer enrolled sports heroes from rugby (Vares and Braun 2006, 325). Likewise, a television ad in New Zealand has featured a couple riding a motorbike on a sheep farm with the woman driving (Vares and Braun 2006, 318). How this advertising has been localized for the Swedish context says much about how and to whom Viagra is marketing itself in Sweden, and about what stereotypical images of masculinity and gender relations it feels are legitimate to base such a campaign on. Perhaps our results are surprising for a nation that prides itself on gender equality. These images can also be read as suggestions of what concepts of masculinity are so stable and unassailable that they can withstand association with a drug that is, in essence, an acknowledgement of 'failed' masculinity and 'dysfunctional' sexuality. Or, as Vares and Braun call it, 'a pill not only to repair, but also to enhance or improve, both erectile functioning and masculinity' (Vares and Braun 2006, 325). As such, the online imagery of the Swedish Viagra man provides a telling account of naturalized Swedish masculinity as intersected by sexual orientation, ethnicity, age and class. And, like the work of Mamo and Fishman, our analysis has shown that Viagra is a gendered drug, 'transmitting cultural scripts which serve as enforcers of normatively gendered expressions of sex and sexuality' (Mamo and Fishman 2001, 20). According to the international Viagra script, male sexuality is always active and desirous, the on-demand erected penis is central in its penetrative function (Potts and Tiefer 2006, 268–9), and according to the Swedish site, the Viagra man can easily be transposed into a different national context, sustaining its hegemonic, naturalized and nationalized image of the common (or, rather common-ized) 'Svensson' who in effect is not so anonymous or unmarked but visibly heterosexual and white, while haunted by blue yearnings of sexual un-fulfilment. He is associated with a wide, middle-class socioeconomic group, one which has the capital to access the seaside and take holidays in the Swedish archipelago, perhaps using the peaceful nights there to dream about tax deductions.

In spite of the mythical figure created online of the ordinary Swedish Viagra man, users of Viagra come in many shapes, sizes, ages, classes and genders. In addition, internationally, there are less than positive stories about using Viagra (Grace *et al.* 2006), reflected in the fact that at least half of Viagra customers do not refill their prescriptions – which is a statistic also found in Swedish studies of Viagra users (Ströberg *et al.* 2006). Further, an interview study by Potts and colleagues (2004) suggests that the importance of bodily experience of both erection and impotence is far more complex. Interviewees in that study challenged medical definitions of the meaning of sexual function as well as the straightforward link between Viagra and a satisfying sexual life. Instead, reports were given of how erectile difficulties led to more gratifying intimate relations by expanding the sexual repertoire. Some even reported how the use of Viagra, contrary to being a quick fix for relationships, affected sexual relationships for the worse.

At the same time, alternative uses of Viagra, not least of all by women, have come to light, suggesting that as Viagra is integrated into our understandings of sexual practice, it becomes a flexible medical technology that means different things to different people. Viagra discourse is symptomatic of sociocultural imaginaries that are glocally situated, as these involve branding techniques and marketing strategies that breach distinctions between public and private (even intimate), health and commerce. While widely promoted as a pharmaceutical success and a scientific breakthrough, Viagra is also a symbolic materialization of the commodification of sexuality and gender, health and old age. It is in this sense that the Viagra imaginary is important to study (and by implication then take part in and intervene into) as it provides an indicator of embodied subjectivities as they take shape.

Notes

1 An earlier version of this chapter has been published as Åsberg, C. and Johnson, E. (2009). Viagra Selfhood: Pharmaceutical Advertising and the Visual Formation of Swedish Masculinity. *Health Care Analysis*, *17* (2), 144–59.

2 Accessed in October 2007, February and April 2008, November 2009 and October 2015.

3 See the special issue of *Sexualities*. *Sexualities*, *9* (3), 2006.

4 Intersectionality accounts for how identities are never just sexed and gendered, but also conditioned by nationhood, ethnicity and racialization, class and so forth. An analytical insistence on intersectionality emerged from within the social sciences and antiracist feminist theory (Haraway 1989; McClintock 1995; Davis 2008). In that vein, we argue that the educational advertising of Viagra in Swedish in fact does more than merely provide information. It generates cultural negotiations over gender and sexuality as these are intersected by issues of, for instance, age and ability, nationhood and ethnicity.

5 All translations are the authors'.

6 Lyrics and melody by Thomas Ledin.

8 Conclusions

Glocal pharma and the Swedish Viagra man

Ericka Johnson

In this book we have been looking at how pharmaceuticals are localized in a specific context: in Sweden, with its well-developed, Northern/Western medical system and the welfare policies that provide this medical system at very little point-of-contact cost to the majority of people living there.

Specifically, we have analyzed the presence and influence of Viagra through the theoretical lens of pharmaceuticalization, as Williams and colleagues (2011a) described. Following their lead, we look at pharmaceuticals even '*outside* the medical domain and explore the broader way in which pharmaceutical *futures* are shaping how we think about innovation, policy and the very meaning of health and illness, therapy and enhancement' (Williams *et al.* 2011b; 730 emphasis in the original). We have paid particular attention to three aspects: the way pharmaceuticals change forms of governance and are changed themselves by local policies; the redefinition of health problems as issues with a pharmaceutical solution; and the creation of new techno-social identities around drugs and the way pharmaceuticals become essential actors in relationships between subjects. Doing so, we see quite clearly that Viagra and its perceived threat of eventually emptying the state coffers by over-demand has been part of a discussion that changed the way pharmaceuticals are subsidized and governed (and govern) in Sweden. Viagra has redefined impotence in the Swedish context as erectile dysfunction, and been presented as *the* solution available through medical treatment. While this is not a process that has only happened in Sweden, the medical discourse around it has incorporated aspects of pharmaceutical treatment that are particularly relevant in a context which provides subsidized medicine. Finally, as the last two chapters showed, Viagra has created a 'Swedish Viagra man' drawing on unique – if stereotypical – Swedish masculinities. Viagra has also been placed as an essential element in this man's relationships with sexual partners and doctors.

Our work in this book has focused on discourses, but the carrier or medium of those discourses is sometimes text, visual images and the materialities of the pills themselves. Our approach to discourse, and the subjects one can read from it, is framed by science and technology studies (STS) understandings of relational agency and non-human actors. These understandings allow us to articulate the role of Viagra as an actor in processes of pharmaceuticalization, but we are also keen to show – as the previous chapters have done – that other (human) actors and (policy and commercial) interests and structures are implicated in pharmaceuticalization, too. Articulating pharmaceuticals in the local context with these theoretical concerns helps us show specific aspects of global pharmaceuticals as they are refracted in Sweden. Here, in the final chapter, we would like to present the reader with an analysis of glocal pharma through the trope of the Swedish Viagra man, to give form to these glocal manifestations of pharmaceuticalization.

The Swedish Viagra man

We have used Viagra as a prism through which to observe the glocal aspects of pharmaceuticalization. Cultural and social studies of Viagra in other contexts have shown how it influences more than just blood flow in the penis. Viagra has introduced the term *erectile dysfunction* (ED) to the general public, changing how impotence is perceived and treated (Chapter 4; Bordo 1998; Marshall 2002; Loe 2004a; Tiefer 2006). It has reinforced a coital imperative – the idea that all sex and intimacy must involve penetrative intercourse – stressing quick, hard (youthful) erections and constant male desire (Tiefer 2000, 2006; Fishman and Mamo 2001; Mamo and Fishman 2001; Marshall 2002, 2006; Potts 2004; Loe 2004b), and it has connected successful ageing with successful sex and successfully taking one's medications (Marshall and Katz 2002; Moynihan and Cassels 2005; Marshall 2006). Yet much of the critical work about Viagra comes from the North American context, where DTC advertising has been widespread and overpowering (Elliot 2003; Moynihan and Cassels 2005). In our work, we have asked how Viagra has influenced ideas about disease, sex and pharmaceutical use in this small, peripheral country, Sweden, with its laws against DTC advertising of prescription drugs, with state-funded, universal health care and a history of, or at least a reputation for, sexual freedom. Taking a look at 'downstream' effects of pharmaceutical science, we show that the specific structural characteristics of the health care system and the cultural landscape influence how Viagra acts and is received in Sweden. We use the figurative Swedish Viagra man in our analysis to represent a subject position which is facilitated, described and prescribed by the multitude of local and global responses to Viagra as it is called into being in the Swedish context and discourse. This figure sits at the juncture of the Swedish state, Swedish cultural identity (as it is imagined, not necessarily as it *is*), the internationally acclaimed pharmaceutical product and the consumer(s) of it (see Johnson *et al.* 2011).

State subsidies and ED

Who should pay for the Viagra man's Viagra? This question has generated heated debate, both in the United States (should insurance companies pay for Viagra but not birth control pills?) and in Sweden (what if a huge public demand drains the state coffers?). Historically, government regulation has often been seen as part of the process to bolster medical expertise (Starr 1982; Petryna and Kleinman 2006). As medical practices were regulated by the state, they were simultaneously granted legitimacy and positioned against traditional medicine and unscientific cures. Likewise, the development of regulated medical schools and the licensing practices they facilitate creates legitimate experts out of medical doctors. 'The increased standardization of the therapeutic process was believed to promote scientific progress in medicine while protecting the public against inflated claims about the effects and uses of substances claimed as remedies to restore health. One unintended effect of such regulation has been that it works as a barrier to market entry for prescription drugs – thus ensuring profits for those who are allowed to enter' (Petryna and Kleinman 2006, 10).

In the discussion about Viagra's subsidy debate in Sweden (Chapter 2), however, we detailed an example of this happening, but in a nuanced way that responded to local concerns and structures. In 2003, the newly formed Swedish Pharmaceutical Benefits Board decided that Viagra would not be subsidized. Doctors could prescribe Viagra, but the Swedish Viagra man would have to pay for it himself. The decision was controversial because people in Sweden had, until then, been accustomed to receiving prescription medication free, past a basic co-pay level, and Pfizer promptly appealed the decision. During the course of the next few years, the question of Viagra subsidies made its way through a series of court cases and appeals until, in 2008, the Supreme Court upheld the initial decision. Today, Viagra is still not subsidized in Sweden.

The Pharmaceutical Benefits Board was convinced subsidizing Viagra would be a legitimate use of tax money for *severe* ED but not for *mild* ED. However, it was also convinced that patients would claim to suffer from the severe form of the disease to beguile doctors into prescribing subsidized Viagra, which would both give subsidies to men who really did not deserve them, and lead to diagnostic bracket creep, that is an expansion of the diagnostic categories to match medication. Thus, rationalized both the Benefits Board and the court, it would be better not to subsidize the drug at all. The decision reflected concerns about patient and doctor compliance with government policies. The clincher in their argument was that two other drugs against severe ED, one injected by syringe into the penis and one inserted as a stick into the urethra, were already subsidized in Sweden. According to the Benefits Board and the court, these two drugs are so unpleasant to administer, compared to taking a pill, that men with mild ED would not reasonably be expected to use them, *de facto* limiting their subsidized use to 'legitimate' patients with severe ED.

In the discourse the state (represented by the regulatory agency) presented in court documents, medical doctors were presented as invalid experts, as easily beguiled individuals who could not diagnose a patient correctly. And the resulting regulation removed the responsibility to diagnose severe erectile dysfunction from the medical expert, placing it instead with the pharmaceutical and its delivery method, a clear example of what Biehl terms *pharmaceutical forms of governance* (Biehl 2006, 218). As predicted, this regulation had significant effects on which pharmaceuticals were sold and subsidized, working as a market entry barrier (although probably not a particularly effective one; see Chapters 4 and 5). The unsubsidized Swedish Viagra man was influenced by the particular local structural framework of the Swedish welfare state.

Chapters 2 and 3 of this book show that the regulatory changes we noted were a response to pharmaceuticals, especially Viagra. Analyzing the court documents that followed Viagra through the long and arduous series of court cases surrounding the decision (finally upheld) to not subsidize it in Sweden, we saw that the regulatory body tasked with deciding about pharmaceutical subsidies in Sweden was producing very local, nation state–specific responses to the integration of international pharma within an allegedly culturally neutral, objective, scientific, medical knowledge paradigm. This regulatory board was, of course, working within an international (European) regulatory framework, but its decisions were influenced by cultural aspects of the Swedish medical system. A new drug – Viagra – and a new regulatory body led to new regulatory tools. Because of local peculiarities like the uneven distribution of urologists throughout the country and the political ideology of the health care system's framework with the principle of equal access to health care guaranteed by law, the drug precipitated a debate and decision about subsidy based on structural and ideological aspects of the Swedish health care system. The glocal of Viagra provision became inseparable from the local context of the regulatory body.

Chapter 3 then discussed how this Swedish government agency, the Pharmaceutical Benefits Board, has tried to include or exclude certain other prescription drugs from the national pharmaceutical benefits scheme. By looking at cases which involve ambiguous knowledge, the chapter showed how regulatory bodies appreciate stable objects and stable categories, both of patients and diseases, and of pharmaceutical treatments. When technology destabilizes these things, as new pharmaceuticals do, and as pharmacogenomics technologies threaten to do even more, the regulatory bodies have to find ways of reacting to unstable categories. How this is done can vary from nation state to nation state, even within a collective framework like the EU, which is striving towards regulatory harmonization. In Sweden, we have seen a tendency to disregard specific knowledge and inclusion criteria and instead use broadly inclusive or exclusive categories for treatable patients and reasonable drugs.

The impotent Swedish man and his dysfunctional penis

In our analysis of impotence and ED in the Swedish medical literature, using the weekly trade journal *Läkartidningen*, we noted a distinct change before and after Viagra's 1998 introduction. Prior to Viagra, impotent men were written about as a heterogeneous group: some had partners, others were older, single men; some were shy, young men with problems relating to women, others were men 'with a secret', although what that secret could be was never clearly articulated. The treatment options for these various patients differed, but the doctor was always supposed to be a trusting confidant who saw the man on several occasions, listened to his feelings and discussed his concerns. Furthermore, the patient's partner was encouraged to be involved in these discussions because she (the partner was always imagined to be a woman in this literature) could play an important role in the man's treatment. After the introduction of Viagra to Sweden, the partner almost disappeared from the medical discourse. So did the term *impotence*. Instead, *erectile dysfunction* was discussed, an affliction of the man's penis, a disease of blood flow and tissues rather than an illness related to relationships, feelings, expectations and disappointments (which has also been seen in other national contexts; see Tiefer 2006). Since 1998, Viagra has dominated the Swedish medical discourse so completely that its availability determined the concept of the patient (reduced to a penis) and the disease (a biomechanical shortcoming) in the medical discourse. Not until 2006, when statistics showed more than half of the men prescribed Viagra in Sweden chose not to refill their prescriptions, was this discourse undermined. Reporting on interviews with men who stopped taking Viagra, an article in *Läkartidningen* suggested that Viagra failed because of social, cultural and relationship issues, unwittingly bringing the discussion back to the relationship and lifestyle causes of impotence that had been prominent in the early 1990s. But this article is the exception to the rule. Viagra today still dominates the way impotence/ED is defined and treated in the Swedish *Läkartidningen*: impotence has become erectile dysfunction and is a condition to be treated pharmaceutically.

Addressing this aspect of pharmaceuticalization in Chapters 4 and 5, we demonstrate the way health problems which already had a medical solution, that is were already medicalized, became issues with a pharmaceutical solution at a glocal level in the Swedish medical discourse. We analyzed how Viagra and alpha-blockers for BPH (Viagra is often prescribed together with alpha-blockers because of side effects of the alpha-blockers) were discussed in the Swedish medical journal *Läkartidningen*. We also paid close attention to who was allowed to give voice to concerns about the use of Viagra and alpha-blockers. Distinct global trends were visible in the Swedish material, like in the construction of impotence and erectile dysfunction as a condition related solely to blood flow after the introduction of Viagra. Discussions shifted from social and relationship causes of impotence to mechanical and biomedical explanations in Sweden as in other Western/Northern countries. Specifically Swedish aspects of the Viagra (and alpha-blocker) medical discussion were also prominent, many related to the solidarity principle in Swedish health care. These aspects included debates about the (un)availability of urologists in different parts of the country, the right a patient has to the best care regardless of his geographical location, the extent to which erections were an aspect of health that should be provided by state-funded medicine (and who was the patient in such cases, the man or the partner), and the connection between erectile dysfunction and other serious medical conditions which had already been deemed justified to treat from the public purse.

Viagra has (largely) replaced sexual and relationship therapy for the Swedish Viagra man, and it far outsells other, earlier, more mechanical solutions like pumps, implants and insertable sticks. The alpha-blockers discussed in Chapter 5, on the other hand, have not had this same effect on treatment options. To some extent, alpha-blockers have become a pharmaceutical solution to a medical problem – enlarged prostates – that previously relied on surgery to correct, but not nearly as completely as Viagra took over erectile dysfunction. In Sweden today, surgeons still perform large numbers of surgeries on benign prostate hyperplasia.

So while alpha-blockers are being prescribed to shrink the prostate more than they were twenty years ago, they have not completely pharmaceuticalized this already medicalized problem in the same way Viagra did. Analyzing the discourse in *Läkartidningen* and comparing it to that of Viagra, one thing that strikes us is that the authorship of articles about impotence/erectile dysfunction shifted dramatically with the introduction of Viagra, from being dominated by sex therapists to being dominated by urologists. But within the discourse on enlarged prostate treatments, urologists were always the main authors of articles in *Läkartidningen*. The introduction of alpha-blockers to the enlarged prostate treatment regime did not imply a change in which medical specialty claimed the disease. Perhaps this can in part explain why the original treatment, surgery, is still performed. Rather than shifting care site, the pharmaceuticals merely added another weapon to the arsenal at the urology clinic. The relative success of Viagra compared to alpha-blockers may have more to do with the relative strengths and weaknesses of urology surgeons and sexologists as professional groups than the drugs themselves. Viagra has wrestled customers away from the sexologists, but alpha-blockers are having a more difficult time taking prostate operation patients away from the urology surgeons.

Commercial images of the Swedish Viagra man

The discursive contours of the Swedish Viagra man's subject position become very clear in the commercial marketing material for Viagra in Sweden. Pharmaceutical marketing has received a good deal of academic attention, in both its pure form as advertisements (see Moynihan and Cassels 2005) and its more subtle forms, like clinical trials, ghost-written scientific articles, medical activism by supported patient groups and disease awareness campaigns (Healy 2006, 62). The marketing of pharmaceuticals is international in its scope, and our Swedish material featured many characteristics which were similar to, for example, marketing produced for the United States. However, there were also distinctions. While these similarities and differences are interesting in detail (and are discussed in Chapters 6 and 7), what we find more relevant to an analysis of pharmaceuticalization is how the marketing discourses created both diseases and subjects which and who are then both actively produced and produce action through their relationship to the drugs. As Healy succinctly notes, 'companies now sell diseases rather than just drugs' (Healy 2006, 82). Our material supports this and shows that the concept of 'consumer' must also be viewed as flexible. Pharmaceuticals enrol and enable relationships to sell their diseases and drugs. Such advertisements target not only the person injecting, ingesting or applying the product, but also the person's family, doctor, school, job or prison facility suggesting, encouraging, prescribing or mandating consumption.

Most DTC advertising of prescription medicine is forbidden in Sweden, so instead of using television commercials, pharmaceutical companies provide information about drugs and medical conditions in pamphlets distributed by doctors and nurses, through supporting patient advocacy groups and on informational websites – a useful way to circumvent DTC rules, according to industry insiders, and seen in other contexts, too (Applbaum 2006, 103–4). This sort of advertising is a clear example of the selling of sickness which can occur; the construction of an illness with a pharmaceutical solution that Moynihan and Mintzes (2010) and Williams and colleagues (2009; 2011a) discuss. Pharmaceuticals are often presented to the patient together with online quizzes that can be used for self-diagnosis or for diagnosis in the clinical setting. These quizzes are frequently translated and appear on websites in many different languages and for many different diseases (erectile dysfunction, depression, benign prostate hyperplasia, female sexual dysfunction, to name a few).

When we analyzed the images of men that populate the Pfizer-funded, Swedish-language webpage about ED, we saw examples of both global harmonization and local adaptation. Much of the information about ED is similar to that found in US commercial material, but the Swedish Viagra man as a collective trope is a slightly different man than the one(s) found in the United States. He is, for starters, very white – which mirrors a traditional image of the Swedish man even though Sweden is, at this point, a country which has a significant non-Caucasian population – and the Swedish Viagra man is slightly older than the middle-aged men and sports stars found as Viagra representatives in the United States. The Swedish Viagra man is also very connected to nature; he is presented in wilderness scenes, toughing the winter cold or jumping into pristine water from rugged, stony outcroppings. The Swedish Viagra man is comfortable in the uncivilized wilderness, which by association naturalizes both his condition and its cure, Viagra.

We also notice that the Swedish Viagra man is not alone in his affliction; he is accompanied by his partner. Images of smiling women next to their men, couples walking along the seaside and two sets of feet sticking out from under a blanket pepper the websites and informational literature. While the partner all but disappeared from the *medical* discourse when Viagra appeared in Sweden, she (there is little to suggest homosexual relationships in the material, even if the language is gender neutral) is actively enrolled and present in the *commercial* material. We suspect this is because Viagra needs sexual stimulation to function properly. For some men and in some cases, Viagra will ensure the maintenance of an erection, but initial sexual stimulation has to come from somewhere or someone else, and the partner is a convenient ally for Pfizer.

The Swedish Viagra man does not act in solitude, and in Chapter 6 we have shown how Viagra is used to create three subject positions in the commercial/informational discourse: a shy and reluctant Swedish Viagra man; his helpful doctor who represents science and knowledge and who is concerned about his patient's impotence in part because of what it says about his patient's heart and general health status; and a supportive partner who can facilitate and produce the nearness and intimacy that a loving, sexual relationship needs.

Chapter 7 paid closer attention to the representations of masculine traits that are given to the Swedish Viagra man within the pages of the Pfizer-sponsored website providing health information on erectile dysfunction to potential Swedish Viagra customers. We have articulated the images of a potential Swedish Viagra man in relation to sexual health and cultural cues of masculinity. We argue that the masculine traits highlighted in the webpages are indicative of Swedish cultural values of male virility that are strong enough to withstand discursive coupling with a pharmaceutical used to address 'failed' virility.

In both of these chapters, the global and the local are relevant as the websites and informational pamphlets we have analyzed are local adaptations of international marketing approaches (including the self-help quiz and the database of local, Viagra-friendly doctors) and are produced and distributed within a regulatory framework that (more or less successfully) forbids DTC advertising of prescription pharmaceuticals. They therefore provide a glocalized cultural imaginary of Viagra, the subject positions it engenders and the particular relationships it facilitates.

Glocal pharma

Pharmaceuticals and the commercial forces behind them are incredibly flexible and determined in their drive to conquer new markets and ensure a global reach (Petryna and Kleinman 2006, 7). However, we also see in our material that the local can push back. Cultural-specific discourses can be and are incorporated into ideas about the consumer subject, and perhaps this is testimony to their obduracy. Medical professionals and opinion makers address the integration of pharmaceutical solutions into clinical practice and treatment, and while many of them may be enthusiastic supporters and/or be receiving pharmaceutical industry support, not all are. Their participation in this discourse is also testimony to a belief that their locally generated opinions are useful, valid and objective. Likewise, the industry supports their role as independent opinion makers with valuable expert advice to be considered by policymakers and other political and administrative bodies. Both industry's use of local doctors and the doctors' willingness to participate attend to a belief that the local is relevant. And that regulatory bodies in a small nation state like Sweden still feel that they have a duty to the citizen (the citizen patient and the citizen taxpayer), which should be considered before the industry's demands, and a court system which facilitates this, attests to the relational agency that develops as global drugs meet local structures.

As we mentioned in the introduction, in drawing conclusions about the glocal of pharmaceuticalization, it is useful to ask how a drug's presence has altered the concept of a disease and its treatment, who suffers from it and how to cure it, in the local context and internationally. Drugs can both create new and refract with existing stereotypical images of a patient, images which carry markers of class, race and sexuality. And they lead to new laws and policies to regulate the practices of both doctors and patients.

But of course it is not only the *drug* that prescribes behaviours or identities, it is decision makers, commercial actors and medical experts who attach the drug to specific demands, images and expectations to influence the behaviours of groups they are trying to govern, cajole or cure. These actors are located in different countries, have different cultural starting points and work within different institutional frameworks, so how they construct and use a pharmaceutical varies. Thus, the series of Swedish court cases and subsidy debates about Viagra reflect the specifics of Swedish law, its national health care programme and its basis in the concept of solidarity. This becomes a framework which creates a specific, local legal context within which Viagra must be governed, and which also influences the discursive contours of Viagra in Sweden. While Viagra's influence on the medical discourse in Sweden was similar to the international one, it also contained a great deal of debate about the connection of ED to other established medical conditions like diabetes and MS, reflecting the subsidy controversy and concern that Viagra would be unavailable to 'legitimate' patients. Likewise, the commercial construction of Viagra on Pfizer's Swedish webpage in many ways parallels that on the US pages, with a self-help diagnostic quiz, a database of Viagra-friendly doctors and information for partners. Yet there are also specific elements manipulated to reflect and resonate with Swedish sensibilities, like the imagined race of the user, the connection to Swedish forests and coastlines and the Swedish survey of masculine personality traits on the Pfizer-sponsored Swedish potency website. These details show a global pharmaceutical being localized.

When an analysis of pharmaceuticalization teases out the actors behind a drug, one can see that a drug is much more than the pill that is claimed to cure a disease or alleviate a symptom. It can become a discursive conflation of values, actors, structures, biomedical understandings, social identities and personal desires. The mere existence of a pharmaceutical product can influence the medical discourse, reinforce and even construct cultural ideas and identities, change the practices of experts and lay people and reimagine ways relationships are performed between patients and doctors and between patients and their loved ones (see Whyte *et al.* 2006). Pharmaceuticals are global in their reach and regulated by international institutions, but our work here articulates drugs as flexible artefacts as they encounter local social and institutional frameworks. While there are very Swedish aspects of Viagra in Sweden, the drug has carried with it previously established ideas about disease, medical treatments for ageing and appropriate intimacy practices. These are strong, disciplining discourses that influence even as they become embedded in the cultures that encounter them. The globalization of the pharmaceutical market not only makes medicines available to international consumers, it also spreads ideas about the healthy subjectivities those medicines are prescribing. This, we feel, calls for further consideration, to articulate the prescribed subjectivities that prescription medicines carry when they are sold on a globalized pharmaceutical market. We want to consider the images of healthy identities, relationships and practices they claim to facilitate. We also call for careful attention to the local particularities they challenge and are challenged by: the medical structures that provide access to them; the ideological basis of local health care provision; and the regulatory frameworks that govern them. These are the local aspects we have examined which, when combined with a global pharmaceutical, relationally construct *glocal pharma*. A question this awakes is if, and how, these local productions of pharmaceutical artefacts and subject positions can be seen to inform backwards, from the peripheral local to the industry's centre.

References

Aarden, E. (2009). *Politics of Provision: The Co-production of Genetic Technologies and Health Care Arrangements in Germany, the Netherlands and the United Kingdom*. Maastricht: Maastricht University.

Abraham, J. (2010). Pharmaceuticalization of Society in Context: Theoretical, Empirical and Health Dimensions. *Sociology 44* (4), 602–22.

Abraham, J. (2011). Evolving Sociological Analyses of Pharmaceuticalization: A Response to William, Martin and Gabe. *Sociology of Health and Illness, 33* (5), 726–8.

Abraham, J., and Ballinger, R. (2012). The Neoliberal Regulatory State, Industry Interests and the Ideological Penetration of Scientific Knowledge: Deconstructing the Redefinition of Carningens in Pharmaceuticals. *Science and Technology & Human Values, 37* (5), 442–77.

Abraham, J., and Lewis, G. (2000). *Regulating Medicines in Europe: Competition, Expertise and Public Health*. London, New York: Routledge.

Aldstedt, E. (1998). Viagra sälgs olagligt via postorder. *Läkartidningen, 95* (51–2), 5859.

American Psychiatric Association (1980) *Diagnostic and Statistical Manual of Mental Disorders* (3rd edn). Washington, DC: American Psychiatric Association.

American Urological Association (AUA). (2010). *American Urological Association Guideline: Management of Benign Prostate Hyperplasia(BPH)*. Linthicum, MD: AUA Education and Research.

Anderson, B. (1983). *Imagined Communities: Reflections on the Origin and Spread of Nationalism*. London and New York: Verso.

Applbaum, K. (2006). Educating for Global Mental Health: The Adoption of SSRIs in Japan. In A. Lakoff, A. Petryna and A. Kleinman, *Global Pharmaceutical: Ethics, Markets, Practices* (pp. 85–110). Durham, NC: Duke University Press.

Application for Subsidy: Levitra, 8369–04 (Kammerräten I Stockholm December 2004).

Åsberg, C. (2005). *Genetiska Föreställingar: Mellan genus och gener i populär/vetenskapens visuella kulturer*. Linkjöping: Linkjöping University Press.

Åsberg, C., and Johnson, E. (2009). Viagra Selfhood: Pharmaceutical Advertising and the Visual Formation of Swedish Masculinity. *Health Care Analysis, 17* (2), 144–59.

Aucoin, M., and Wassersug, R. (2006). The Sexuality and Social Performance of Androgen-deprived (Castrated) Men Throughout History: Implications for Modern Day Cancer Patients. *Social Science and Medicine, 63*, 3162–73.

Baglia, J. (2005). *The Viagra Adventure: Masculinity, Media and the Performance of Sexual Health*. New York: Peter Lang.

Balint, M. (1957). *The Doctor, His Patient and the Illness*. London: Pitman.

Becker, H., Geer, B. and Hughes, E. (1961). *Boys in White: Student Culture in Medical School.* Chicago: Chicago University Press.

Beerman, B. (2000). Rabattering är en politisk fråga. *Läkartidningnen, 97* (8), 870.

Beerman, B. (2003). Läs rekommendationerna! *Läkartidningen, 100* (21), 1918.

Berg, M. (1997). *Rationalizing Medical Work: Decision Support Techniques and Medical Practices.* Cambridge: MIT Press.

Bergstörm, L. (1998). Potensmedel tar USA med storm. *Läkartidningen, 95* (25), 2927–9.

Berner, B., and Johnson, E. (2010). *Technologies and Medical Practices: Blood, Guts and Machines.* Surrey: Ashgate.

Biehl, J. (2006). Pharmaceutical Governance. In A. Lakoff, A. Petryna and A. Kleinman, *Global Pharmaceuticals: Ethics, Markets, Practices* (pp. 206–39). Durham, NC: Duke University Press.

Bijker, W. E. (1995). *Of Bicycles, Bakelites and Bulbs: Towards a Theory of Sociotechnical Change.* Cambridge: MIT Press.

Bodlund, O. (2008). Sildenadil hjälper även kvinnor med sexuella biverkningar av SSRI. *Läkartidningen, 105* (43), 3005.

Bordo, S. (1998). Pills and Power Tools. *Men and Masculinities, 1* (1), 87–90.

Braidotti, R. (2006). *Transpositions: On Nomadic Ethics.* Cambridge: Cambridge Polity Press.

Branke, K. (1998). Allehanda om Parjehanda. En personlig refleksjon äver USA's nya potensdebatt. *Läkartidningen, 95* (25), 3016.

Brody, H. (2007). *Hooked: Ethics, the Medical Professional and the Pharmaceutical Industry.* Lanham, MD: Rowman & Littlefield.

Brunsson, N., and Jacobsson, B. (2000). *A World of Standards.* Oxford: Oxford University Press.

Bryld, M., and Lykke, N. (2000). *Cosmodolphins: Feminist Cultural Studies of Technology, Animals and the Sacred.* London: Zed Books.

Butler, J. (1990). *Gender Trouble: Feminism and the Subversion of Identity.* New York: Routledge.

Byström, J. (2000a). Impotensmedicin på 'nöjeskontot'? *Läkartidningen, 97* (3), 214.

Byström, J. (2000b). Visst rekommenderar Läkarmedelsverket. *Läkartidningen, 97* (8), 870.

Callon, M. (1987). Society in the Making: The Study of Technology as a Tool for Sociological Analysis. In W. E. Bijker, T. P. Hughes and T. J. Pinch, *The Construction of Technological Systems* (pp. 83–103). Cambridge: MIT Press.

Callon, M., and Law, J. (1995). Agency and the Hybrid Collectif. *South Atlantic Quartely, 94*, 481–507.

Carlsson, P., and Spångberg, A. (1996a). Dyra, nya läkemedel batter än kirugi? *Läkartidningen, 93* (49), 4549–55.

Carlsson, P., and Spångberg, A. (1996b). Har Patienten Rätt att Välja. *Läkartidingen, 93* (49), 4556–8.

Castor-Vázquez, G. (2006). The Politics of Viagra: Gender, Dysfunction and Reproduction in Japan. *Body and Society, 2* (2), 109–29.

Casula, Å. V., and Sjögren, E. (2011). More Knowledge, Better Government? Consequences of Knowledge-based Decision Making in Swedish Pharmaceutical Benefits. *Governance, 24* (1), 85–110.

Ciechanowski, S. (1903). *Prostatic Hypertrophy: Anatomical Researches on the So-called 'Prostatic Hypertrophy' and Allied Processes in the Bladder and Kidneys.* Translated by E. R. Pelton. Krakow: University of Krakow.

Christensen, T., and Lægreid, P. (2002). *New Public Management: The Transformation of Ideas and Practice*. Aldershot: Ashgate.

Claridge, J. A., and Fabian, T. C. (2005). History and Development of Evidence-based Medicine. *World Journal of Surgery, 29* (5), 547–53.

Clarke, A., Mamo, L., Fishman, J. and Shim, J. (2010). *Biomedicalization, Technoscience, Health and Illness in the U.S.* Durham, NC and London: Duke University Press.

Conrad, P. (2007). *The Medicalization of Society.* Baltimore, MD: Johns Hopkins University Press.

Coser, R. L. (1963). Alienation and the Social Structure: Case Analysis of a Hospital. In Eliot Freidson, *The Hospital in Modern Society* (pp. 231–265). London: The Free Press.

Cuyler, A., and Newhouse, J. (2000). *Handbook of Health Economics.* Amsterdam: Elsevier.

Dahlstrand, C. (2003) Ett bra och säkert terapival – för både patienten och sjukvården. *Läkartidningen, 100* (35), 2678.

Davis, K. (2008). Intersectionality as Buzzword. A Sociology of Science Perspective on What Makes a Feminist Theory Successful. *Feminist Theory 9* (1), 67–85.

Dawson, G. (1994). *Soldier Heroes: British Adventure, Empire and the Imagining of Masculinities*. London and New York: Routledge.

Degerblad, M., Elmér, C., Falconer, C., Jonasson, A. F., Lauritzen, M. and Lökk, J. (2014). Nokturi-en underdiagnostiserad och ofta obehandlad folksjukdom. *Läkartidningen, 1111: CUWD.*

Dervieux, T., and Bala, M. V. (2006). Overview of the Pharmacoeconomics of Pharmacogenetics. *Pharmacogenomics, 7* (8), 1175–84.

Drori, G., Meyer, J. W., Ramirez, O. F. and Schofer, E. (2003). *Science in the Modern World Polity: Institutionalization and Globalization.* Stanford, CA: Stanford University Press.

Dugdale, A. (2000). Intrauterine Contraceptive Devices, Situated Knowledges and the Making of Women's Bodies. *Australian Feminist Studies, 15* (32), 165–76.

Dumit, J. (2012). *Drugs for Life: How Pharmaceutical Companies Define Our Health.* Durham, NC: Duke University Publishing.

Eaton, J., and Weil, R. (1955). *Culture and Mental Disorders.* Glencoe, IL: The Free Press.

Egalite, O. N., and Godard, B. (2007). Pharmacogenomics Research Involving Racial Classification: Qualitative Research Findings on Researchers' Views, Perceptions and Attitudes Towards Socioethical Responsibilities. *Pharmacogenomics*, *8* (9), 1115–26.

Ekman, P. (1999). Många behandlingsalternatiiv vid prostathyperplasi. *Läkartidningen, 96* (34), 3504–5.

Elam, M. (2012). Pharmaceutical Incursion on Cigarette Smoking at the Birth of the Brain Disease Model of Addiction. In J. Netherland, *Critical Perspectives on Addiction: Advances in Medical Sociology* (Vol. 14, pp. 53–75). London: Emerald Press.

Elliott, C. (2003). *Better Than Well. American Medicine Meets the American Dream.* New York: W.W. Norton and Company.

Elvin-Nowak, Y. and Thomsson, H. (2001). Motherhood Is Idea and Practice. A Discursive Understanding of Employed Mothers in Sweden. *Gender & Society, 15* (3), 407–28.

European Association of Urology (EAU). (2006). Guidelines on Benign Prostate Hyperplasia. Arnhem, NL: European Association of Urology.

Fall, M. (1999). Urininkontinens hos mannen-ett försummat problem? *Läkartidningen, 96* (18), 2227–31.

Fishman, J. (2004). Manufacturing Desire: The Commodification of Female Sexual Dysfunction. *Social Studies of Science*, *34* (2), 187–218.

Fishman, J., and Mamo, L. (2001). What's in a Disorder: A Cultural Analysis of Medical and Pharmaceutical Constructions of Male and Female Sexual Dysfunction. *Women & Therapy, 24* (1/2), 179–93.

Flowers, C. R., and Veenstra, D. (2004). The Role of Cost Effectiveness Analysis in the Era of Pharmagenomics. *PharmacoEconomics, 22* (8), 481–93.
Foucault, M. (1987) [1976]. *The History of Sexuality. An introduction*. Translated by Robert Hurley. New York: Penguin Books.
Foucault, M. (2007). *Security, Territory, Population: Lectures at the College de France, 1977–1978*. Basingstoke: Palgrave Macmillan.
Foucault, M. (2008). *The Birth of Biopolitics: Lectures at the College de France, 1978–1979*. Basingstoke: Palgrave Macmillan.
Fox, R. (1959). *Experiment Perilous: Physicians and Patients Facing the Unknown*. Glencoe, IL: The Free Press.
Fox, R. (1977). The Medicalization and Demedicalization of American Society. *Daedalus, 106* (1), 9–22.
Fox Keller, E. (1992). *Secrets of Life, Secrets of Death: Essays on Language, Gender and Science*. New York: Routledge.
Franklin, S., Lury, C. and Stacey, J. (2000). *Global Nature, Global Culture*. London, Thousand Oaks, and New Delhi: Sage Press.
Freidson, E. (1963). *The Hospital in the Modern Society*. London: The Free Press.
Friberg, T. (2006). *Diagnosing Burn Out: An Anthropological Study of a Social Concept in Sweden*. Lund: Lund University.
Fuberg, C. (2003a). Minska förskrivningen av dyra läkemedel utan mervärde. *Läkartidningen, 100* (49), 4113.
Fuberg, C. (2003b). Alfadil-positiv dokumentantation för säkerhet saknas. *Läkartidningen, 51–2*, 4329.
Ginsburg, G., Konstance, R., Allsbrook J. and Schulman, K. (2005). Implications of Pharmacogenomics for Drug Development and Clinical Practice. *Archives of Internal Medicine, 165* (20), 2331–6.
Grace, V., Potts, A. Gavey, N. and Vares, T. (2006). The Discursive Condition of Viagra. *Sexualities, 9* (3), 295–314.
Gray, A., and Harrison, S. (2004). *Governing Medicine: Theory and Practice*. London: Open University Press.
Gunnarsdotter, S. (2005). Erektil dysfunktion kan tyda på hjärt-kärlsjukdom. *Läkartidningen, 102* (36), 2458.
Gurwitz, D. Z., Hopkins, M. M., Gaisser, S. and Ibarreta, D. (2009). Pharmacogenetics in Europe: Barriers and Opportunities. *Public Health Genomics, 12* (3), 134–41.
Hacking, I. (1999). *The Social Construction of What?* Boston, MA: Harvard University Press.
Hallin, A. (1999). Produktutvekling efterlyses för termoterapi vid prostataförstoring. *Läkertidningen, 96* (34), 3520–2.
Hansen, A. (2006). Nytt preparat mott för tidig utlösning. *Läkartidningen, 103* (40), 2943.
Haraway, D. (1989). *Primate Visions: Gender, Race and Nature in the World of Modern Science*. New York: Routledge
Hart, N., Grand, N. and Riley, K. (2006). Making the Grade: The Gender Gap, ADHD, and the Medicalization of Boyhood. In D. Rosenfeld and C. A. Faircloth, *Medicalized Masculinities* (pp. 132–64). Philadelphia, PA: Temple University Press.
Hassler, E. (2002). Att behandla prostatiker i primärvård inte enkelt-trots frågeformulär. *Läkartidningen, 99* (19), 2174.
Healy, D. (2004). *Let Them Eat Prozac. The Unhealthy Relationship between the Pharmaceutical Industry and Depression*. New York: New York University Press.
Healy, D. (2006). The New Medical Oikumene. In A. Lakoff, A. Petryna and A. Kleinman, *Global Pharmaceuticals: Ethics, Markets, Practices* (pp. 61–84). Durham, NC: Duke University Press.

Healy, K. (2000). Embedded Altruism: Blood Collection Regimes and the European Union's Donor Population. *American Journal of Sociology, 105* (6), 1633–57.

Hedelin, H. (1998). Nytt medel mot impotens. *Läkartidningen, 95* (42), 4558–60.

Hedelin, H. and Abramsson, L. (1997). Vem Skall Behandla Erektil Dysfunktion? *Läkaretidningen 94* (28–9), 2548–52.

Hedelin, H., Grenabo, L. and Holmäng, S. (2001). Både stora genombrott och stagnation inom urologin. *Läkartidningen, 98* (20), 2440–4.

Hedelin, H., and Jacobsson, L. (2000). Viagra förstahandsmedel mot erektil dysfunktion. *Läkartidningen, 97* (21), 2616–17.

Hedelin, H., Johansson, N. and Ströberg, P. (2003). Ojämn kvalitet på remisser för blåstomningensproblem hos män. *Läkartidningen, 100* (16), 1435.

Hedgecoe, A. (2002). Reinventing Diabetes: Classification, Division and the Genetization of Disease. *New Genetics and Society, 21* (1), 7–27.

Hedgecoe, A. (2004). *The Politics of Personalized Medicine-pharmacogenetics in the Clinic. Cambridge*: Cambridge University Press.

Hedgecoe, A. (2008). From Resistance to Usefulness: Sociology and the Clinical Use of Genetic Tests. *BioSocieties, 3* (2), 183–94.

Hedgecoe, A., and Martin, P. (2003). The Drugs Don't Work: Expectations and the Shaping of Pharmacogenetics. *Social Studies of Science, 33* (3), 327–64.

Heyns, C. F., and de Klerk, D. P. (1989). Pharmaceutical Management of Benign Prostatic Hyperplasia. In D. Paulson, *Prostatic Disorders*. London: Lea & Febiger.

Hirschauer, S. (1998). Performing Sexes and Genders in Medical Practices. In A. Mol and M. Berg, *Differences in Medicine: Unraveling Practices, Techniques and Bodies* (pp. 13–27). Durham, NC: Duke University Press.

Hopkins, M. M., Ibarreta, D., Gaisser, S., Enzing, C., Ryan, J., Martin, P., Lewis, G., Detmar, S., Elske van den Akker-van Marle, M., Hedgecoe, A., Nightingale, P., Dreiling, M., Hartig, K., Vullings, W. and Forde, T. (2006). Putting Pharmacogenetics into Practice. *Nature and Biotechnology, 24* (4), 403–10.

Hopkins, M. M., Martin, P. A., Nightingale, P., Kraft, A. and Mahdi, S. (2007). The Myth of the Biotech Revolution: An Assesment of Technological, Clinical and Organizational Change. *Research Policy, 36* (4), 566–89.

Hult, E. (2006). Vetenskap i paketerad form: Framväxten av evidensbaserad medicine. In C. Waks, and C. Levay, *Sträven efter transparens: Gransking, styring och organisering i sjukvårdens nätverk* (pp. 77–100). Stockholm: SNS Förlag.

Illich, I. (1976). *Limits to Medicine/Medical Nemesis: The Expropriation of Health*. London: Marion Boyars.

Järhult, B. (2005). Pfizer uppmanas svara på kritik och delta i det offentliga samtalet. *Läkartidningen, 100*.

Järhult, B., and Lindahl, S.-O. (2003). 'Blodtrycksmaffians' agerande har kostat skattebetalarna milijarder. *Läkartidningen, 100* (22), 1917–18.

Jasanoff, S. (2004). *States of Knowledge: The Co-production of Science and Social Order*. London: Routledge.

Jasanoff, S. (2005). *Designs on Nature: Science and Democracy in Europe and the United States*. Princeton, NJ: Princeton University.

Johansson Krafve, L. (2015). *Valuation in Welfare Markets: The Rulebooks, Whiteboards and Swivel Chairs of Care Choice Reforms*. Linköping: Linköping University.

Johnson, E. (2008). Chemistries of Love: Impotence, Erectile Dysfunction and Viagra in the *Läkartidningen. Läkartidningen, NORMA 3* (1), 31–47.

Johnson, E., and Åsberg, C. (2012). Enrolling the Swedish Viagra Man. *Science and Technology Studies*, *25* (2), 46–60.

Johnson, E., and Sjögren, E. (2009). Conniving Patients, Beguiled Doctors and Disciplining Drugs: Justifying the Denial of Reimbursment for Viagra Use in Sweden. *Paper Presented at the 6th Nordic Medical Anthropology Conference*. Gothenburg, Sweden.

Johnson, E., Sjögren, E. and Åsberg, C. (2011). Prescribing the Swedish Viagra Man. *Clinical Pharmacology and Therapeutics*, A Nature Publication. January.

Jordanova, L. (1999). *Nature Displayed: Gender, Science and Medicine 1760-1820*. London: Longman.

Jost, T. (2005). *Health Care Coverage Determinations: An International Comparative Study*. Maidenhead: Open University Press.

Junker, S.-O. (2014). Att Skapa gemenskap: hur beslut fattas i en EU myndighet. PhD Dissertation. Stockholm: Stockholm School of Economics.

Källström, R. (2010). *Construction, Validation and Application.* Linkjöping: Linkjöping University Press.

Kammarrätten in Stockholm (Stockholm Administrative Court of Appeals). (2005). *Application for Subsidy: Viagra.* Case no. 5014-04. Issued 15 April 2005.

Kassirer, J. (2005). *On the Take: How Medicine's Complicity with Big Business Can Endanger Your Health.* Oxford: Oxford University Press.

Kimland, E., and Ståhle, L. (2004). Läkemedelsfrågan. *Läkartidningen, 101* (35), 2666–7.

Kirby, R., Fitzpatrick, J., Kirby, M. and Fitzpatrick, A. (1995). *Delat Ansvar för prostata sjukdomar.* Stockholm: Merck Sharp.

Kirchheiner, J., Fuhr, U. and Brockmoller, J. (2005). Pharmacogenetics-based Therapeutic Recommendations – Ready for Clinical Practice? *Nature Reviews Drug Discovery, 4* (8), 639–47.

Kruse, C. (2016). The Social Life of Forensic Evidence. Oakland: University of California Press.

Lagrelius, A. M., and Sjögren, E. (2004). Reglers mångfold: Läkemedelsreglering i Sverige. In G. Ahrne and B. Nils, *Regelexplosionen* (pp. 93–125). Stockholm: EFI.

Lakoff, A. (2005). *Pharmaceutical Reason: Knowledge and Value in Global Psychiatry.* Cambridge: Cambridge University Press.

Lakoff, A. (2006). High Contracts: Gifts and Surveillance in Argentina. In A. Lakoff, A. Petryna and A. Kleinman, *Global Pharmaceuticals: Ethics, Markets, Practices* (pp. 111–35). Durham, NC: Duke University Press.

Landtblom, A.-M. (2004). Stöd permanent rabatt av Viagra och Cialis vid MS! *Läkartidningen, 101* (35), 2666–7.

Landtblom, A.-M. and Ertzgaard. P. (2000). Tillstånded – inte läkemedlet – ska avgöra frågan om subventionering. *Läkartidningen, 97* (21), 2612–14.

Länsrätten in Stockholm (Stockholm County Administrative Court). (2004a) *Application for Subsidy: Viagra.* Case no. 8032-03. Issued 30 June 2004.

Länsrätten in Stockholm (Stockholm County Administrative Court). (2004b) *Application for Subsidy: Cialis.* Case no. 11092-03. Issued 30 June 2004.

Latour, B. (1993). *The Pasteurization of France*. Translated by Alan Sheridan. Cambridge: Harvard University Press.

Latour, B. (1998). On Recalling ANT. Published by the Department of Sociology, Lancaster University, at www.comp.lancs.ac.uk/sociology/papers/Latour-Recalling-ANT.pdf (accessed 4 April 2008).

Law, J. (2006). *Big Pharma: How the World's Biggest Drug Companies Control Illness*. London: Constable and Robinson.

Law, J., and Singleton, V. (2005). Object Lessons. *Organization, 12* (3), 331–5.

Lesko, L. J., and Woodcock, J. (2004). Translation of Pharmacogenomics and Pharmacogenetics: A Regulatory Perspective. *Nature Reviews Drug Discovery, 3* (9), 763–9.

Lindbom, A. (2002). Dismantling the Social Democratic Welfare Model? Has the Social Welfare State Lost Its Defining Characteristics? *Scandinavian Political Studies, 24* (3), 171–93.

Lindén, L. (2013). 'What do Eva and Anna have to Do with Cervical Cancer?' Constructing Adolescent Girl Subjectivities in Swedish Gardasil Advertisements. *Girlhood Studies, 6* (2), 83–100.

Lindgren, G. (1999). *Klass, kön och kirurgi: relationer bland vårdpersonal i organisationsförändringarnas spår*. Malmö: Liber.

Ling, T., and Raven, A. (2006). Pharmacogenetics and Uncertainty: Implications for Policy Makers. *Studies in History and Philosophy of Science, 37* (3), 533–49.

Loe, M. (2004a). *The Rise of Viagra: How the Little Blue Pill Changed Sex in America*. New York: New York University Press.

Loe, M. (2004b). Sex and the Senior Woman: Pleasure and Danger in the Viagra Era. *Sexualities, 7* (3), 303–26.

Lohm, L., and Lindh, E. (2003). Älder och nyare hypertonimedel har likvärdig effekt. *Läkartidningen, 100* (21), 1920.

Löwy, I. (2010). HPV Vaccination in Context: A View from France. In K. Wailoo, J. Livingston, S. Epstein and R. Aronoqitz, *Three Shots at Prevention: The HPV Vaccine and the Politics of Medicine's Simple Solution* (pp. 270–91). Baltimore, MD: John Hopkins University Press.

Löwy, I. (2015). Norms, Values and Constraints: The Case of Prenatal Diagnosis. In I. Dussauge, C.-F. Helgesson and F. Lee, *Values Practices in the Life Sciences & Medicines* (pp. 186–205). Oxford: Oxford University Press.

Lundberg, P. O. (1995). Sexualliv och Läkemedel. *Läkartidningen, 92* (28–9), 2742–7.

Marshall, B. (2002). 'Hard Science': Gender Constructions of Sexual Dysfunction in the 'Viagra Age'. *Sexualities, 5* (2), 131–58.

Marshall, B. (2006). The New Virility: Viagra, Male Aging and Sexual Function. *Sexualities, 9* (3), 345–62.

Marshall, B., and Katz, S. (2002). 'Forever Functional': Sexual Fitness and the Ageing Male Body. *Body & Society, 8* (4), 3–70.

Martin, E. (1991). The Egg and the Sperm: How Science Constructed a Romance Based on Stereotypical Male-Female Roles. *Signs, 16* (3), 485–501.

Martin, E. (1992). *The Woman in the Body: A Cultural Analysis of Reproduction*. Boston, MA: Beacon Press.

Marting, S. J. (1903). *Prostatic Hypertrophy from Every Surgical Standpoint by George M Philips, M.D. and Forty Distinguished Authorities*. St. Louis, MO: The Ajod Company Medical Publishers.

Marx, F. J., and Karenberg, A. (2009). History of the Term Prostate. *The Prostate, 69*, 208–13.

May, C, Rapley, T., Moreira, T, Finch, T. and Heaven, B. (2006). Technogovernance: Evidence, subjectivity, and the clinical encounter in primary care medicine. *Social Science and Medicine, 62* (4):1022–30.

McClintock, A. (1995). *Imperial Leather: Race, Gender and Sexualities in the Colonial Context*. London, New York: Routledge.

Mclaren, A. (2007). *Impotence: A Cultural History*. Chicago: University of Chicago Press.

Mellgren, A. (1993). Ny Behandling of Impotens Review of the Book Pyschomastik der Impotenz by D Langer, U Hartmann. *Läkartidningen, 90* (10), 984.

Merchant, C. (1980). *The Death of Nature: Women, Ecology and the Scientific Revolution.* San Francisco, CA: Harper and Row.

Miller, P., and Rose, N. (2008). *Governing the Present: Administering Economic, Social and Personal Life*. Cambridge: Polity Press.

Mitton, C., and Donaldson, C. (2004). *Priority Setting Toolkit: A Guide to the Use of Economics in Healthcare*. London: BMJ Publishing Group.

Mol, A. (2002). *The Body Multiple: Ontology in Medical Practice.* Durham, NC: Duke University Press.

Mol, A., and Berg, M. (1998). *Differences in Medicine: Unraveling Practices, Techniques and Bodies*. Durham, NC: Duke University Press.

Moreira, T. (2010). When are Trials Not Enough? Clinical Versus Cost-effectiveness in the Controversy Over Access to Dementia Drugs in the NHS. In Catherine Will and T. Moreira, *Medical Proofs, Social Experiments: Clinical Trials in Shifting Contexts* (pp. 85–102). Farnham: Ashgate.

Moynihan, R., and Cassels, A. (2005). *Selling Sickness: How Drug Companies are Turning Us All into Patients.* Crows Nest, Australia: Allen & Unwin.

Moynihan, R., and Mintzes, B. (2010). *Sex, Lies and Pharmaceuticals: How Drug Companies Plan to Profit from Female Sexual Dysfunction.* Crows Nest, Australia: Allen & Unwin.

New Pharmaceutical Benefits Bill (2001). Submitted to Parliament on 13 December 2001. Available from the Swedish Government, www.regeringen.se/sb/d/108/a/1435.

Nightingale, J., and Martin, J. (2004). The Myth of the Biotech Revolution. *Trends in Biotechnology, 22* (11), 564–9.

Nilsson, P., Hedner, T., Himmelmann, A., Kahan, T. and Menhem, K. (2003). Samarbete med industrin önskvart och nödvandigt-med bevarad integritet. *Läkartidningen, 100* (21), 1919.

Oelke, M., Bachmann, A., Desczeuad, A., Emberton, M., Gravas, S., Michel, M. C., N'dow, J., Nordling, J. and de la Rosette, J. J. (2013). EAU Guidelines on the Treatment and the Follow-up of Non-neurogenic Male Lower Urinary Tract Symptoms Including Benign Prostatic Obstruction. *European Urology, 65* (1), 118–40.

Oliffe, J. (2005). Constructions of Masculinity Following Prostatectomy-Induced Impotence. *Social Science & Medicine, 60* (2005), 2249–59.

Oliffe, J. (2006). Embodied Masculinity and Androgen Deprivation Therapy. *Sociology of Health & Illness, 28* (4), 410–32.

Olsson, A. M., Abramsson, L., Höjerback, T., Malmberg, L. and Pedersen, J. (1995). Är det Möjligt att bota impotens? *Läkartidningen, 92* (4), 313–16.

Olsson, A. M., Forsberg, L., Höjerback, T. and Nilsson, A. (1990). Impotens på grund av arteriell insufficiens kan ha funktionella orsaker. *Läkartidningen, 87* (51–2), 4456.

Örn, P. (2001). Fler får dispens för lakemedel mot fetma. *Läkartidningen, 98* (47), 5294.

O'Shea, C. (2012). 'A Plea for the Prostate': Doctors, Prostate Dysfunction, and Male Sexuality in Late 19th- and Early 20th-Century Canada. *Canadian Bulletin of Medical History CBMH/BCHM, 29* (1), 7–27.

Oudshoorn, N. (1994). *Beyond the Natural Body: An Archeology of Sex Hormones*. London: Routledge.

Oudshoorn, N. (1997). Menopause Only for Women? The Social Construction of Menopause as an Exclusively Female Condition. *Journal of Psychosomatic Obstretrics and Gynecology, 18*, 137–44.

Oudshoorn, N. (2003). *The Male Pill: A Biography of a Technology in the Making.* Durham, NC: Duke University Press.

Parsons, T. (1951). *Social Structure and Dynamic Process: The Case of Modern Medical Practice.* London: Routledge.

Payne, K., and Shabaruddin, F. H. (2010). Cost-effectiveness Analysis in Pharmacogenomics. *Pharmacogenomics, 11* (5), 643–6.

Pendergast, M. K. (2008). Regulatory Agency Consideration of Pharmacogenomics. *Experimental Biology and Medicine, 233* (12), 1498–503.

Petryna, A. (2006). Globalizing Human Subjects Research. In A. Lakoff, A. Petryna and A. Kleinman, *Global Pharmaceuticals: Ethics, Markets, Practices* (pp. 1–32). Durham, NC: Duke University Press.

Pharmaceutical and Dental Benefits Agency. (2008a, December 12). Application for Subsidy: Levitra (online) 2004. Retrieved from www.tlv.se.

Pharmaceutical and Dental Benefits Agency. (2008b, December 12). Application for Subsidy: Viagra (online) 2003.

Pharmaceutical and Dental Benefits Agency. (2008c, December 12). Application for Subsidy: Viagra (online). Stockholm County Administrative Court 2004.

Pharmaceutical Benefits Board. (2003a, January 30). *Autonativ.* Stockholm, Sweden. Retrieved from www.tvl.se.

Pharmaceutical Benefits Board. (2003b, January 30). *Robinul.* Stockholm, Sweden. Retrieved from www.tvl.se.

Pharmaceutical Benefits Board. (2003c, March 26). *Viagra.* Stockholm, Sweden. Retrieved from www.tvl.se.

Pharmaceutical Benefits Board. (2003d). *Caverjet.* Stockholm, Sweden. Retrieved from www.tvl.se.

Pharmaceutical Benefits Board. (2003e). *Bondil.* Stockholm, Sweden. Retrieved from www.tvl.se.

Phillips, K. A., Veenstra, D., Ramsey, S., van Bebber, S. and Sakowski, J. (2004). Genetic Testing and Pharmacogenomics: Issues for Determining the Impact to Healthcare Delivery and Costs. *American Journal of Managed Care, 10* (7), 425–32.

Phillips, K. A., and Van Bebber, S. L. (2006). Regulatory Perspectives on Pharmacogenomics: A Review of the Literature on Key Issues Faced by the United States Food and Drug Administration. *Medical Care Research and Review, 63* (3), 301–26.

Plante, R. (2006). Review of Loe, Meika, *The Rise of Viagra: How the Little Blue Pill Changed Sex in America. Sexualities, 9* (3), 379–80.

Pope, C. (2003). Resisting Evidence: The Study of Evidence-based Medicine as a Contemporary Social Movement. *Health, 7* (276), 267–82.

Porter, T. M. (1995). *Trust in Numbers: Objectivity in Science and Public Life.* Princeton, NJ: Princeton University Press.

Potts, A. (2004). Deleuze on Viagra (Or, What can a 'Viagra-Body' Do?). *Body & Society, 10* (1), 17–36.

Potts, A., Gavey, N., Grace, V. and Vares, T. (2003). The Downside of Viagra: Women's Experiences and Concerns. *Sociology of Health and Illness, 25* (7), 697–719.

Potts, A., Grace, V. and Gavey, N. (2006). Sex for Life? Men's Counter-stories on 'Erectile Dysfunction', Male Sexuality and Ageing. *Sociology of Health & Illness, 28* (3), 306–29.

Potts, A., Grace, V., Gavey, N. and Vares, T. (2004). Viagra Stories: Challenging 'Erectile Dysfunction'. *Social Science & Medicine, 59*, 489–99.

Potts, A., and Tiefer, L. (2006). Introduction. *Sexualities, 9* (3), 267–72.

Power, M. (1997). *The Audit Society: Rituals of Verification.* Oxford: Oxford University Press.

Prainsack, B. (2007). Research Populations: Biobanks in Israel. *New Genetics and Society, 26* (1), 85–103.

Prainsack, B., and Firestine, O. (2006). Science for Survival: Biotechnology Regulation in Israel. *Science and Public Policy, 33* (1), 33–46.

Premfors, R., Ehn, P., Haldén, E. and Sundstöm, G. (2003). *Demokrati och byråkrati (Democracy and Bureaucracy).* Lund: Studentlitteratur.

Raj, A. K. (2002). Pharmacogenetic Interventions, Orphan Drugs and Distributive Justice: The Role of Cost Benefit Analysis. *Social Philosophy & Policy, 19* (2), 246–70.

Rappert, B. (2001). The Distribution and Resolution of the Ambiguities of Technologies or Why Bobby Can't Spray Bobby Can. *Social Studies of Science, 31* (4), 557–91.

Reardon, J. (2004). *Race to the Finish: Identity and Governance in an Age of Genomics.* Princeton, NJ: Princeton University Press.

Regeringsrätten. (2008a, March 14). Judgement in the Case 2713–05 Concerning the Subsidization of Viagra.

Regeringsrätten. (2008b, March 14). Judgement in the Case 2716–05 Concerning the Subsidization of Cialis. 5.

Regeringsrätten. (2008c, March 14). Judgement in the Case 2719–05 Concerning the Subsidization of Levitra.

Reidy, J. (2005) *Hard Sell: The Evolution of a Viagra Salesman.* Riverside, NJ: Andrews McMeel Publishing.

Rose, N. and Novas, C. (2005). Biological Citizenship. In A. Ong and S. Collier, *Global Assemblages: Technology, Politics and Ethics as Anthropological Problems* (pp. 439–463). Oxford: Blackwell.

Sandberg, L. (2011). *Getting Intimate: A Feminist Analysis of Old Age, Masculinity & Sexuality.* Linköping: LiU Tryck.

SBU Swedish Council on Health Technology Assessment (Statens Beredning for Medicinsk utvärdering) (2011). Godartad Prostataförstoring med avflödeshinder (Benign Prostate Hyperplasia with Flow Restrictions). *Rapport 209.*

Sengoopta, C. (2006). *The Most Secret Quintessence of Life.* Chicago and London: The University of Chicago.

Shackley, D. (1999). A Century of Prostatic Surgery. *BJU International, 83,* 776–82.

Shenkin, B. (1973). Politics and Medical Care in Sweden: The Seven Crowns Reform. *New England Journal of Medicine, 288,* 555–9.

Sjögren, E. (2006). Reasonable Drugs: Making Decisions with Ambiguous Knowledge. Dissertation. Stockholm: Stockholm School of Economics.

Sjögren, E., and Fernler, K. (2010). Democratic Priority-setting? Organizing Multiple Stakeholders to Make Decisions in the Healthcare Sector. In L. Sonderyd, G. Sundström and S. Furusten, *Organizing Democracy: The Construction of Agency in Practice* (pp. 94–112). Cheltenham: Edward Elgar.

Sjöstrand, M. (1998). Förbattring av erektionssvikt oftast bra för två personer! *Läkartidningen, 95* (46), 5139.

Socialutskottet. (1997). Socialutskottets betänkende 1996/97: SoU14. *Prioritetingar inom hälso och sjukvården.* Swedish Goverment.

Spångberg, A., and Dahlgren, H. (2013). Godartad prostataförstoring med avflödeshinder. *Läkertidningen, 110* (13–14), 682–5.

Stacey, J. (1997). *Teratologies. A Cultural Study of Cancer.* London and New York: Routledge.

Stacey, J. (2000). The Global Within: Consuming Nature, Embodying Health. In S. Franklin, C. Lury and J. Stacey, *Global Nature, Global Culture* (pp. 97–145). London, Thousand Oaks and New Delhi: Sage Press.

Star, S. (1991) Power, Technology, and the Phenomenology of Conventions: On Being Allergic to Onions. In J. Law, *A Sociology of Monsters: Essays on Power, Technology and Domination* (pp. 22–56). London: Routledge.

Star, S. L., and Bowker, G. C. (1999). *Sorting Things Out: Classification and Its Consequences*. Cambridge: MIT Press.

Starr, P. (1982). *The Social Transformation of American Medicine*. Cambridge: Basic Books.

Stockholm County Administrative Court (2004). Application for Subsidy: Viagra. Available from: www.tlv.se (Accessed 12 December 2008), www.tlv.se/Upload/Ovrigt/OVR_050418_dom_KR_viagra.pdf (Issued 15 April 2005).

Stöckl, A. (2010). Public Discourses and Policy Making. The HPV Vaccination from the European Perspective. In K. Wailoo, J. Livingston and S. Epstein, *Three Shots at Prevention: The HPV Vaccine and the Politics of Medicine's Simple Solutions* (pp. 254–69). Baltimore, MD: John Hopkins University Press.

Ströberg, P., Hedelin, H. and Bergström, A. (2006). Sex-bara för rika och friska? *Läkartidningen, 103* (39), 2865–6.

Ströberg, P., Hedelin, H. and Ljunggren, C. (2006). Behandling av erektil dysfunktion med PDE-5 hämmare. *Läkartidningen, 103* (14), 1107–11.

Swedish Book of Statutes (SFS). (1982:763). The Health and Medical Service Act. Retrieved from www.regeringen.se/sb/d/108/a/23172.

Swedish Book of Statutes (SFS). (2001, April 2). Act on Pharmaceutical Benefits. Retrieved from www.notisum.se/rnp/sls/lag/20020160.HTM.

Swedish Book of Statutes (SFS). (2001/140, April 2). *Förordning om ändring i förordningen(1996:1294) om högkostnadsskydd vid köp av läkemedel m.m.* Retrieved from www.notisum.se/rnp/sls/fakta/a9961294.htm.

Swedish Parliament. (2001, December 2001). *New Pharmaceutical Benefits Bill.* Retrieved December 12, 2008, from www.regeringen.se: www.regeringen.se/sb/d/108/a/1435.

Tiefer, L. (2000). Sexology and the Pharmaceutical Industry. *The Journal of Sex Research, 37* (3), 273–94.

Tiefer, L. (2006). The Viagra Phenomenon. *Sexualities, 9* (3), 273–94.

TLV (2003). Application for Subsidy: Viagra. Available from: www.tlv.se (Accessed 12 December 2008), www.tlv.se/Upload/Beslut/BES_030326_Viagra.pdf (Issued 26 March 2003).

TLV (2005). Genomgången av läkemedel mot migrän. Available from: www.tlv.se, www.tlv.se/Upload/Genomgangen/rapport-migran.pdf (Accessed 12 December 2008).

TLV (2006). Genomgången av läkemedel mot sjukdomar orsakade av magsyra. Available from: www.tlv.se, http://www.tlv.se/Upload/Genomgangen/rapport-magsyra.pdf (Accessed 12 December 2008).

Timmermans, S., and Berg, M. (2003). *The Gold Standard: The Challenge of Evidence-based Medicine and Standardization in Health Care*. Philadelphia. PA: Temple University Press.

Vares, T., and Braun, V. (2006). Spreading the Word, But What Word Is That? Viagra and Male Sexuality in Popular Culture. *Sexualities, 9* (3), 315–32.

Wagstaff, A., Van Doorslaer, E., Van der Burg, H., Calonge, S., Christiansen, T., Citoni G., Gerdtham, U-G, Gerfin, M., Gross, L. and Hakinnen, U. (1999). Equity in the Finance of Health Care: Some Further International Comparisons. *Journal of Health Economics, 18*, 263–90.

Wailoo, K., Livingston, J. and Epstein, S. (2010). *Three Shots at Prevention: The HPV Vaccine and the Politics of Medicine's Simple Solutions.* Baltimore, MD: Johns Hopkins University Press.

Whyte, S. R., Whyte, M. A., Lotte, M. and Kyaddondo, B. (2006). Treating AIDS: Dilemmas of Unequal Access in Uganda. In A. Petryna, A. Lakoff and A. Kleinman, *Global Pharmaceuticals: Ethics, Markets, Practices* (pp. 240–62). Durham, NC: Duke University Press.

Willems, D. (1998). Inhaling Drugs and Making Worlds: A Proliferation of Lungs and Asthmas. In M. Berg and A. Mol, *Differences in Medicine: Unraveling Practices, Techniques and Bodies* (pp. 105–18). Durham, NC: Duke University Press.

Williams, R. (1980). *Culture and Materialism. Selected Essays.* London and New York: Radical Thinkers, Verso.

Williams, S. J., Gabe, J. and Davis, P. (2009). *Pharmaceuticals and Society: Critical Discourses and Debates.* West Sussex: Wiley-Blackwell.

Williams, S. J., Martin, P. and Gabe, J. (2011a). The Pharmaceuticalisation of Society? A Framework for Analysis. *Sociology of Health and Illness, 33* (5), 710–25.

Williams, S. J., Martin, P. and Gabe, J. (2011b). Evolving Sociological Analysis of 'Pharmaceuticalisation': A Reply to Abraham. *Sociology of Health & Illness, 33* (5), 729–30.

Witz, A. (1992). *Professions and Partriarchy.* London: Routledge.

Zetterqvist, A., Merlo, J. and Mulinari, S. (2015). Complaints, Complainants, and Rulings Regarding Drug Promotion in the United Kingdom and Sweden 2004–2012: A Quantitative and Qualitative Study of Pharmaceutical Industry Self-Regulation. *12* (2), e1001785 doi:10.1371.

Zetterqvist, A., and Mulinari, S. (2013). Misleading Advertising for Antidepressants in Sweden: A Failure of Pharmaceutical Industry Self Regulation. *PLOS one, 8* (5), 1–12.

Index

For Product Safety Concerns and Information please contact our EU representative GPSR@taylorandfrancis.com Taylor & Francis Verlag GmbH, Kaufingerstraße 24, 80331 München, Germany

Batch number: 10725973

Printed by Printforce, the Netherlands